From users of the Chocolate Model—

Jennifer O'Hartigan, Supervisor Global Training & Design, logistics service provider—*My expectations of a few tips to help me at my job were greatly exceeded. My practitioner toolbox is filled with practical change aids and process steps….Change management used to be an overwhelming and scary term to me. After reading about it, practicing being a change agent…I am confident that I can be a change agent in my organization.*

Christina Pethe, Intermarket Supply Planner, global import-export corporation—*The information on the skills/knowledge plus the personal attributes that a change agent needs to be successful really helped me envision what a change agent should look like and what I personally need to work on to become a better change agent.*

Christa Ledbetter, Disability Advocate, Center for Independent Living—*I have a good foundation of the basic principles of change agentry now. I learned that—Adoption of a change is a flowing process with twists and turns; it rarely goes from A to Z… Adopters are people first, their feelings matter—listen carefully. Learn to understand the organization, what its communication lines are, who the leaders are, why the change is necessary and/or beneficial, which key people will be your champions and where the strengths and weaknesses are.*

Randy Kirk, Organizational Effectiveness Specialist, The Methodist Hospital, Houston, Texas—*I learned that as much as I think "This Change Is Easy" and there should be no problem, there can be many challenges that I have not thought of…This project was small scale compared to the bigger picture and project I am up against this next year…Now I'm ready!*

Nancy Torkewitz, Soft Skills Trainer for 4000+ employees, a global agri-products company—*Completing the assessments [worksheets] never failed to reveal an insight, even though several times when I first looked at an assessment I wasn't sure if it had applicability to my project. Each one did. My other really big takeaway was the insight I got…about whether or not it was OK for the Team to be doing all the work with their fellow adopters while [the change agent] remained mostly in the background, guiding them as to how to be maximally effective…And here I was at the opposite end of the spectrum trying to do it all, rather than relying on others to convey the messages. I was INeffective.*

Marc Donelson, Program Manager, HQ national department store chain—*I definitely have a better understanding of how to communicate new ideas to management. Instead of just going into conversations myself, I need to build a base with opinion leaders in my department.*

Tiffini Sorcic, Learning & Development Consultant, brokerage firm—*The upfront planning…[using the] tools and techniques should yield big dividends when the change implements…*

Lisa Kennedy, Instructional Designer, government agency—*Using these tools will keep me from wasting time and energy by allowing me to focus on the areas that will facilitate or hinder the change…the two most important [things I learned] are …too little information makes people leery about the change and the change agent's credibility. Too much information can be just as bad because they stop listening. I also didn't realize how much impact social networking has…It makes sense that like people would tend to band together on issues or tend to listen more to those that are similar to them. It just wasn't something I had thought about.*

Lt(N) Ginette Lupton, Training Officer, Canadian Navy—*You can't change people; you can help people change by giving them what they need.*

Josephine Poelma, Director of Learning Design & Facilitation, national tax service—*…my focus in the past had always been on "getting the project done" without spending too much thought and effort on the change process. Now, I can see how having a strong foundation in change management can help me implement new performance improvement initiatives more smoothly.*

Holly Kersey, Advocate for Childcare Center, church—*I have built an overall confidence…to present change to those who have more power than I.*

LCDR Marcus Gherardi, Training Officer, US Coast Guard Maritime Law Enforcement Academy—*Probably the biggest thing I learned was how important alignment is for a change to be effective. There are so many components that need to be addressed in order for a change to work…[Also] I need to improve my survival skills and to "listen more than I talk." Sometimes in a military environment, people with the most senior rank tend to talk the most…really it should be the opposite!*

The

Chocolate

Model of Change

Diane Dormant

To Charlie & Julian

IMPORTANT! This book includes 25 worksheets. You can create your own Change Project Workbook by downloading free the worksheets in a convenient 8½ x 11 format from *chocochange.com.*

CONTENTS

PREFACE

Why Another Book on Change? There are hundreds of books on change, so why another? Because this book is unique in bringing together three approaches. First, although anyone dealing with change—whether for themselves or for others—can benefit from the concepts offered, this book is especially designed for mid-level folks with the responsibility for getting others to accept an organizational change. Second, it is theory-based but practitioner-oriented. Third, it offers a tested, step-by-step process for facilitating a change.

1. For Change Agents in the Middle

The best-selling books about organizational change are written by business school faculty or consultants with management or OD perspectives (e.g., John Kotter, Edgar Schein, Rosabeth Moss Kanter, Peter Drucker, Joan Gallos, Daryl Conner). Understandably, these experts direct their messages to the top of the organization and focus on leadership. They address such questions as—What should those in leadership roles say and do to bring about organization-wide change? How well does the proposed change align with strategic goals? While these books contribute value even to those not at the top of the organization, they are far from enough for mid-level staff, managers, consultants, or others who are responsible for organizational changes, even though they have little or no authority over those targeted to accept the changes.

In addition to understanding leadership and organizational alignment, mid-level change agents need to understand the targeted end-users—the potential adopters of the change. Fortunately, another group of researchers and writers from sociology, psychology, and education (e.g., Everett Rogers, Kurt Lewin, Ronald Havelock, Gene Hall) offers substantial guidance for this kind of understanding. They address such questions as—How do those on the receiving end of the change feel and behave? What are their concerns? How does their social network affect their acceptance of the change? How can a change agent facilitate their buy-in?

This book brings together these two separate areas of expertise and provides mid-level change agents with help appropriate to their organizational position.

2. Theory-Based, Practice-Oriented This book also has a characteristic not always present in books about change; it is theory-based, but practitioner-oriented. That is to say, in the details of the Chocolate Model and the related process, I have tried to be true to the most reliable research data and theoretical expertise (referenced in the text and in the End Notes), but I have also tried to translate this data and expertise into practical prescriptions for action. Each chapter addresses some dimension or issue of the change situation and most include a worksheet activity in which you can apply what you've read to your own organizational change. If you complete the activities, you will have a comprehensive *action plan* for your own change project.

3. A Field-tested Model and Process My personal reason for writing this book is because of the positive responses from those who have used the Chocolate Model. They have applied the model to real change projects in a variety of organizations and, as you can read in the preceding testimonials, they have found it to be of value.

HOW YOU MIGHT USE THIS BOOK

Step-by-Step Approach This book is designed so that you can take the same step-by-step approach that has been effective for past users of the Chocolate Model. That is, you can select a real-world change project, then work your way through the book—reading about a topic and completing worksheets to apply what you've read to your own project. Worksheets appear in the book but can also be downloaded free in an 8 ½ x 11 format from

chocochange.com

Team Approach If you are working with others—and, for a project of any size, you should be—you can provide a book for everyone or give mini-presentations based on the chapters and distribute related worksheets. You can then compare and discuss analyses and develop a plan together. (If you are selecting the people you will work with, you might read the chapter on the Change Agent Team first.)

Novel Approach Or you can just read the book—like a novel. That is, you can skip all the worksheets and just read the text.

If You Want to Read More Once you have the conceptual frame provided by the Chocolate Model, you are likely to enjoy reading other books on the topics discussed here. Some are referenced in the End Notes or in relevant chapters. Two books I most recommend are *The Heart of Change* by John Kotter and Dan Cohen and *Diffusion of Innovation* by Everett Rogers. The first is easy-to-read and almost certain to give you ideas for your own change project. The latter is 551 pages long and was first published almost 50 years ago, so you might be put off. But it is now in its fifth edition (2003) and, before you reject it, I suggest you read the reviews by current Amazon readers.

ACKNOWLEDGEMENTS

After 30 years of consulting, teaching, and writing articles about change management, I finally wrote this book as the direct result of a series of e-lectures developed for an online graduate course in Boise State University's Instructional and Performance Technology Department. So my first thanks are to the BSU students who challenged and energized me and made my life more interesting and satisfying.

For his mentoring and patience in dragging me kicking and screaming into the 21st century world of online teaching, as well as for his support and friendship, my thanks to Tony Marker, Professor at BSU. For her expertise in helping me become a better teacher and her support and friendship, my thanks to Joan Middendorf, Associate Director of Campus Instructional Consulting Center at Indiana University. Thanks to both for collaborating on our earlier *Change Mapping Workshop* and to Kathy Byers, Director School of Social Work at IU, for her friendship and collaboration on the even earlier *ABCD Model of Change*.

My thanks to Joe Lee, illustrator extraordinaire. To Carol Rhodes for her fantastic graphics help. To Mary Lou Paurazas for her expert editorial help. To Roger Rhodes, Madeleine Gonin, and Cordah Pearce for their ever-present technical help. And to all of these for their friendship and support.

For the opportunity to teach for 25 years at Indiana University, my thanks to the Department of Instructional Systems Technology and especially to ex-Chair Elizabeth Boling. For the BSU opportunity, my thanks to the Instructional and Performance Technology Department, and especially to Chair Don Stepich and Jo Ann Fenner.

For introducing me to such wondrous places as Indonesia and Liberia, as well as for giving me so many exciting professional experiences, thanks to my mentor and friend, Sivasailam "Thiagi" Thiagarajan. For the sometimes scary, but always exciting, professional opportunities they gave me, my thanks to Lee Meyerson, Arizona State U.; Rad Drew and Mike Kinney, Eli Lilly Pharmaceuticals; Mike Tracy, IU Educational Psychology and Charles Pearce, IU Ergonomics.

For bringing love into my life, my thanks to Howard Levie. For not firing me as their mother and for their continued support and encouragement, my thanks and love to Charlie and Julian.

And my thanks to all of the above for their very real part in this book.

1. Introduction

Every once in a while somebody—a neighbor, my dentist, someone in a Y-class—asks me what I do. When I say, "I teach change management," they pause, look at me curiously and ask, "What's change management?" To me, the answer always seemed obvious— "It's managing change." So for a long time, I couldn't understand why they found the subject to be so odd, so mysterious. Finally, though, I realized that it's not that they see change management as mysterious or complicated. It's just the opposite. They see it as simple, something everyone does. Why would anyone need to learn how to do it?

It's true that everybody does manage change. But often they don't do it very well. Not for themselves, and not when they're managing other people's changes—changes like those that happen every day in organizations. As you can see in this example, it's not always easy to get people to accept new ways—even a new way of approaching change management.

> Some years ago, a colleague and I did a two-day workshop for a group of employees at a large manufacturing plant. They came from training, IT, engineering and several operational departments. The first day, we presented information about what makes a change acceptable, about why people resist change and about the process people go through as they move toward accepting a change. After each segment, the participants worked in teams to apply the content to their own change projects.
>
> That evening, when my co-instructor and I compared notes, we concluded that Day 1 had gone pretty well. Attendees had asked good questions, worked intently on their projects, and—all in all—seemed to be "getting it."
>
> When we arrived early the next morning, two of the participants—engineers— were already waiting for us. After friendly greetings, one of them said, "Diane, the stuff you told us about yesterday is all right, but our question is—How do you _make_ people accept change?"

We realized then that these two had completely missed the whole point of our approach—an approach not about "making," but about "helping," people accept organizational change. Why had they missed our point? One reason was because we had not taken into enough consideration the perspective of an engineer—a professional who is used to problem-solving and designing with components that are more decipherable and controllable than people. We had failed to understand *them* and, at least in part for that reason, they had rejected *our* change. One of the most important skills this book offers is that of how to understand the significant others in an organizational change situation.

My hope is that every reader will look again at managing change— this ordinary thing that everybody does, recognize how complex and difficult it really is and learn how to cope with that complexity and difficulty in a way that will increase the level of success for everyone involved.

Three Ways to Manage a Change

Three ways to manage an organizational change—that is, to get other people to accept the change—are...

- *use force*
- *cause pain*
- *facilitate acceptance*

Use Force

One way to get people to change is to coerce them, force them to act in new ways. This works in prisons (most of the time), but it is not the way a democracy treats its citizens, and it is not the way most successful modern-day organizations treat their employees.

Cause Pain

Another way to get people to change is to cause pain. Make people miserable if they don't change. This is sometimes called the "burning platform" approach.

The Burning Platform

A few years ago out in the North Sea, an oil rig caught on fire. The crew sent a radio distress message, though they doubted the rig would last long enough for help to arrive. As it turned out, they had good reason to worry. By the time the rescue boat got there, out of the 212 people aboard, 123 were dead.

One man was alive because he jumped off the burning platform into the icy water, and the rescuers were able to pull him out before hypothermia killed him. Later when a reporter asked him why he jumped, he said, "Well I knew if I stayed on the burning platform, I'd die. If I jumped, I had a chance.

This story was widely reported in the media and it caught on among people who write about organizational change. As they saw it, the moral of the story was—"If you want people to leave their old ways and move on to new ways of doing things, you need to set fire to the platform under their feet."

This is an interesting idea. Make it uncomfortable for people to stay the same and hopeful for them to change. But, there's a problem with this story-as-metaphor. *Over half of the workers died!* That's a pretty costly way to get a group of people to move.

So when is it appropriate to take such drastic action? Some answers are when…

- there's an emergency
- people are so stuck in their ways, you've got to shake them loose
- the outcome is worth the cost

Even then, consider these suggestions before you set fire to their platform.

1. Communicate the importance of giving up the old way. Be sure the people know the platform under their feet is on fire. And your message must relate to *their* lives, not just to the life of the organization.

2. Communicate the advantage of the new way. Be sure the people know that they have a chance to do better if they jump, if they move on to the new.

3. Station the rescue boats! Successful change agentry involves more than getting people to move. It involves getting them to move in the right direction and as efficiently as possible. If the change is to be effectively used and integrated into the workplace, somebody has to hang around with a "rescue boat" ready—to retrain, coach, encourage, reinforce, whatever is needed.

Facilitate Acceptance

Although there are times when aspects of the "force" or "pain" approaches are appropriate, the best long-term approach—and the one emphasized here—is facilitation. Facilitative change agents involve others as much as possible in the change process. They offer encouragement, information, guidance, support and rewards to those asked to make the change. They know the general principles of change, they see the change from others' perspectives, and they have a reliable model to guide the change process.

General Principles About Change   Knowing—and remembering—these four general principles can help you understand and navigate a change effort.

1. Change is not just an event; it's a *process*.

2. Change takes *time*.

3. Lacking good information, people *horribilize*.

4. Faced with change, people *resist*.

PRINCIPLE 1   Change is not just an event, it's a *process*. There is a tendency to think of a change as an event, but—for the people involved—it is more than an event. It is a *process*. Here's a story to illustrate the point.

Greensburg, Kansas

If you were to look at an aerial photograph of Greensburg, Kansas, taken on May 4, 2007, you would see a town with lots of green trees, rows of tidy white houses, clean streets with cars and trucks, and a main drag with various larger buildings—maybe a school and a feed store. An idyllic, little Midwestern town.

Then if you were to look at an aerial photograph of Greensburg taken the next day, you would see nothing—no trees, no houses, no cars, nothing but rubble. The night before, in just a few minutes, a tornado wiped Greensburg off the face of the earth.

Clearly, this was an event—a devastating one. It took only a few minutes, but for the people of Greensburg, the *process* of change has just begun.

In the days that followed, photographs of the aftermath appeared in the nation's newspapers and television screens. Many showed people picking over the debris, looking for remnants of their former lives.

In one picture, a father, mother, small boy, and a puppy on a leash are walking down the street in front of their destroyed home. The little boy and the puppy have their heads up. They're looking at the photographer with curiosity. The adults, however, are oblivious to the photographer. Heads down, they are already struggling with the loss of their home, their car, their possessions. They are anxious about how they can get something to eat and a place to sleep. They are concerned about their future.

The event is behind them, but these two are just beginning the process of coping with their loss, of meeting their immediate needs, and of figuring out what to do in the weeks and months to come. They are just beginning the *process* of dealing with the change that has been thrust upon them.

Perhaps you're thinking that tornados are not the kind of change you are likely to deal with. Some organizational changes may seem like tornados, but the kind most people deal with are more like these—

NEW...

software systems	*training requirements*
job designs	*environmental developments*
accountability procedures	*government regulations*
facilities	*management*
personnel structures	*production technologies*
programs	*etc.*

Such organizational changes do begin with an event. For example, the announcement of the change. "As of next month, we will be switching over to SAP." "The word just came that our group is being moved to Arkansas." Or a rumor. "Jason just told me we're getting a new boss." The moment when the change is first heard about—that moment is the event.

But the time after the event, the time for dealing with the...

- **loss of what was (PAST)**
- **anxiety about what is (PRESENT)**
- **concerns about what will be (FUTURE)**

...that is the change process we'll be looking at here.

In this kind of situation, what do people need? What are their concerns? How can you help? How can you facilitate their movement through the process of change?

PRINCIPLE 2   Change takes *time*. Whether the change is brought about by something awful or is the promise of something positive, it takes time for people to adjust to and adopt the change. The classic example of this comes from Everett Rogers' *Diffusion of Innovations*.

Hybrid Corn Seed & Midwest Farmers

When it was released in 1928 to Iowa farmers, hybrid corn was an important new technology that offered multiple advantages over seed saved by the farmers from their past crops. The new hybrid corn had been tested and yielded 20%

more per acre, was more resistant to drought, and was easier to harvest mechanically. Sounds like a winner!

But, the first year, the county agents who were assigned to get farmers to adopt the new seed were able to get only a few of the 259 in the state to give the seed a chance and then only on a few acres. Over time, more and more farmers began to see its value and to use the seed until, finally, all but two were using it.

How long did it take? Thirteen years.

Various factors affect how long it takes for people to adjust to a change and we'll look at these later. For now, just be aware that people need *time* to adjust to and adopt a change.

Of course, it's not uncommon for decision makers to create unrealistically short timelines for change projects. The important point is that—regardless of the official timeline—people tend to adopt a change on their own timeline. The effective change agent takes this into consideration.

PRINCIPLE 3   Lacking good information, people *horribilize*. The following story appeared in the newspaper a few years ago when air travel was easy. It's about a proposed change and the images it generated in a small boy's mind.

A Little Boy Faces a Change

For several years, a little boy had been making regular airplane flights back and forth between his divorced parents—his mother in New York City and his father in Los Angeles.

The boy had always looked forward to flying and all of the special attention he got—books, toys, and sometimes a chance to visit the pilot in the cockpit. But this time, several days before he was supposed to leave L.A. for the trip back to his mother, he began to have trouble getting to sleep at night and he started having crying spells. Finally, he just said that he didn't want to go back to New York.

His father called the boy's mother, but she couldn't offer any suggestions. What could possibly be wrong?

On the last night and in the middle of another crying bout, the father asked again what was bothering him. This time, between sobs, the little boy choked out, "Mom said that on the way home, I'd have to change planes. I'm afraid that—when we're up in the air and I have to walk from the wing of the plane to the wing of the other plane—I'm afraid I'll fall off."

While hugging and reassuring the boy, his father explained what "changing planes" really meant.

This story illustrates what can happen when people are asked to make a change they don't understand. In the absence of good information, they think the worst. They *horribilize*.

This little boy was lucky. He had a caring and patient father who observed, listened, asked questions, and offered reassuring and valid information. That's also what a good organizational change agent does—among other things!

PRINCIPLE 4   Faced with change, people *resist*. No matter how good the change is, people are likely to resist. Scott Adams knows this well as he portrays organizational life in his Dilbert cartoons. No matter what the Boss suggests, Dogbert resists.

But even when people don't openly resist, they may subtly or unintentionally resist, as you can see in this anecdote from Brett Christensen of the Canadian Navy.

Sailors Resist a Change

Our Canadian Patrol Frigates were specifically designed to be paperless. But, one of the first things the sailors did when they got onboard was install bookshelves and filing cabinets. The amount of paper that has "crept onboard" has actually changed the weight of the ship enough that the ballast figures had to be reworked.

Whether it's Dogbert or Canadian sailors or just about everyone else, when faced with a change, people *resist*.

See the Change from Others' Perspectives

Remember the old story about the three blindfolded people who approach an elephant and have quite different views. Often when a change is proposed, the designer thinks it's brilliant, the executive sees it as a profit-maker, but the worker who has to use the $%^#&! thing views it as a pain in the neck.

The effective change agent hears and respects all of these viewpoints.

A hose!	A leaf!	A rope!
A brilliant design!	**A profit-maker!**	**A $%^# pain!**

Have a Reliable Model to Guide the Change Process

Managing change is a complex, imprecise endeavor, and a good model can bring order to the process and increase your effectiveness. The model offered here—the Chocolate Model—is research-based, but it is also practical and easy to use, in part or whole, in the real world.

Why Chocolate? Although change is never a "piece of cake," if you understand and plan for four dimensions of your change situation— the *change*, the *adopters*, the *change agent*, and the *organization*—you'll be more effective. The Chocolate Model is organized around these four dimensions.

> **Change** = the new system, process, etc. you want a group of people to accept
>
> **Adopters** = the group targeted to adopt the change
>
> **Change Agent** = YOU and your change team
>
> **Organization** = the organization, or part of the organization, in which all of the above exist

Since model-builders are always looking for memorable acronyms—

Change + Adopters + Change Agent + Organization = CACAO

Cacao is the bean from which chocolate is made. Therefore—the Chocolate Model. An extra benefit of this name is that chocolate is highly palatable to most people, and a change made palatable is one more likely to be accepted.

CACAO ➡ CHOCOLATE MODEL ➡ PALATABLE CHANGE

The following flowchart lays out the steps the book will take you through—all as they relate to your own change project. Your first step is highlighted.

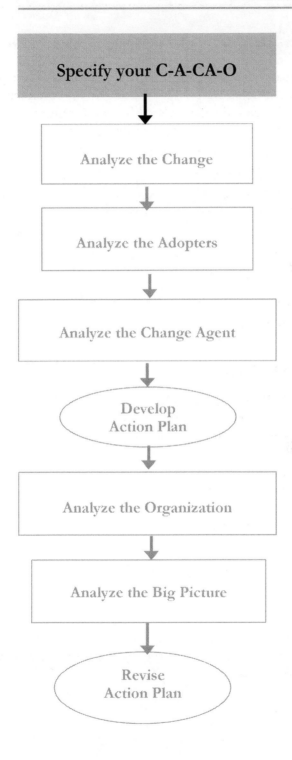

NOTE: For your convenience, worksheets are available free at **chocochange.com.** At this point, I suggest you print out all 25 worksheets to make a complete Change Project Workbook for use throughout the book.

WORKSHEET 1   Select the change project you want to work on throughout the book and specify your C-A-CA-O. That sounds easy, but it isn't always so easy to be specific. (Suggestion: See Appendix A for more detailed instructions and examples of some change projects on which others have worked.)

The CHANGE
The ADOPTERS
The ORGANIZATION

Wherever you record information, it may not be wise to leave worksheets where those—not on your team—have access. Why? Because it's important to be considerate of others' feelings as well as to fulfill any implied or stated promise of confidentiality you may extend as you gather data.

WORKSHEET 2 Self-Assessment Before you read further, think of the change you're going to work on and complete this self-assessment by checking the box that best describes your position at this time. (You'll revisit this at the end.)

	DISAGREE	UNSURE	AGREE
I understand the change fully.			
I personally believe in the change.			
The change is good for the organization.			
The change is good for the users.			
The change can be implemented.			
I am familiar with the users' knowledge of the change.			
I know how the users feel about the change.			
I understand the users' concerns regarding the change.			
I respect the discomfort/pain people feel when asked to change.			
I accept complaints and resistance as natural responses.			
I know the organizational culture well.			
I know how the change relates to current strategy/initiatives.			
I know the sponsor(s) of the change well.			
I know the users' boss well.			
I know how to get resources for this change project.			
Users see me as knowing the change.			
I am accepting of others' viewpoints and opinions.			
I am good at "reading" people.			
Users see me as having their interests in mind.			
Users trust me.			
I am a good stand-up communicator.			
I am a good interviewer.			
I am good at getting others to express their views.			
I am a good writer.			
I listen more than I talk.			
In meetings, I actively participate and communicate my ideas.			
I do not dominate meetings.			
I am good at helping quiet people participate.			
I am good at not letting anyone dominate.			
I am good at defusing or refocusing conflicts.			
I use stress-reducing techniques myself.			
I am confident of my own value apart from this job & project.			
I accept that I alone cannot make this change happen.			
I have family or friends who are good sounding boards.			
I have mentors who give me good organizational advice.			

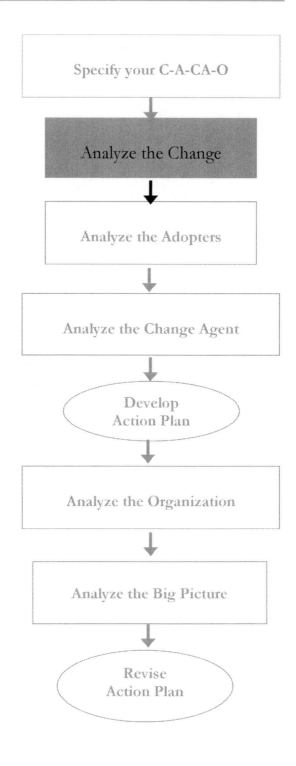

2. The CHANGE

To be effective, the change agent must understand the change. That may seem obvious, but people are often assigned to implement a change they know little about. In fact, sometimes a change project begins before the change has even been fully developed. When this is true, the change agent may have an even more difficult time unless the potential adopters are themselves involved in the development. Here, however, we will assume that the change exists and the change agent's job is to get the adopters to buy in.

However, the fact that the change exists doesn't mean that the adopters know much, if anything, about it. To them, the change is often just a "blackbox."

Although we most frequently hear the term "blackbox" used to refer to a recording mechanism in an airplane or vehicle, there are other uses of the term. One definition is "a device whose internal mechanism is hidden from or mysterious to the user." This is the sense in which the term is used here—to emphasize the adopter's initial lack of knowledge about the change.

Us or Them? There are times when we all feel like it's "us or them." Nowhere is this truer than in a major organizational change. The adopters are sure no one understands their view of the change that is being thrust upon them. As a change agent, you have to remember what it was like when you first heard about the change—when it was just a "blackbox" to you—as it is now to the adopters.

The Ideal Change

What is the ideal change—*from the adopter's point-of-view?*

Researchers[*] differ somewhat in how they describe the characteristics that make a given change acceptable to adopters, but they all agree that certain characteristics do make it more acceptable. Furthermore, they agree that how these characteristics are *communicated* is often critical to the adopters' acceptance of the change.

The Chocolate Model focuses on these five change characteristics:

RELATIVE ADVANTAGE: the change offers advantages over the old way of doing things—*to the adopters*

SIMPLICITY: the change is easy to understand—*by the adopters*

COMPATIBILITY: the change is consistent with past practice—*of the adopters*

ADAPTABILITY: the change can be adapted to fit local conditions—*by the adopters*

SOCIAL IMPACT: the change will have little or no impact on the social relations—*of the adopters*

The repeated emphasis on adopters is no accident. Over and over, you—as a change agent—need to remind yourself to see the change through the eyes of your adopters.

To illustrate how the characteristics of an innovation can affect adoption, here are two examples of trying to get people to adopt new foods.

---

[*] Throughout the book, additional details are given in the End Notes.

A Proposed Change in Food Habits

During World War II, there was a shortage of butter, and the government wanted people to switch to margarine. In those days, margarine was white, and, when you spread it on bread, it looked yukky. So the government wasn't getting anywhere—until somebody figured out that you could add yellow food coloring to margarine and make it look like butter. Sales and use of margarine shot up!

If you evaluate margarine on the five factors listed above, you might get ratings like the following. To individuals, except for the patriotism they felt in wartime, margarine had little or no *relative advantage* over butter. Since the use of margarine was easy to understand, it rated high on *simplicity*. *Adaptability* and *social impact* seem neutral. The problem comes with *compatibility with past practice*. The colorless appearance of margarine, an apparently trivial break with past practice, proved to be a critical barrier to adoption. The person who figured this out and simply made margarine look like butter was an effective change agent.

Here's a more contemporary example from a *Time Magazine* article (paraphrased here). Using our five-item scale, how would you rate this change for American diners?

Dinner's On!

In some parts of the world, insects are a major food source. For example, in Thailand, food markets offer commercially-raised water beetles and bamboo worms. Some argue that insects are a better way to get protein than eating chicken, cows or pigs. Given that livestock is responsible for 18% of the world's greenhouse-gases, insects could be the food of the future.

My guess is that you rated it high on *simplicity* and off the negative end of the scale for *compatibility with past practice*. We may have to reach the desperate stage before we willingly serve bugs for dinner.

Another contemporary example comes from Tom Friedman, *New York Times* columnist and best-selling author, during a Charlie Rose PBS interview.

Rose asked his guest what he thought about our progress in making the world green. Friedman said that so far we are just "playing" at making the necessary changes, that to make serious progress, we need a combination of capital, technology, and public policy. To illustrate the importance of policy, he gave the following example (paraphrased here).

Tom Offers Charlie a Change

Imagine that I invented the first cell phone and I come to you and say, "Charlie Rose, I've got a phone you can carry in your pocket." You'd say, "I can carry it in my pocket! Wow! I'll take ten. For me and for my staff. Because those phones will change my life." I say, "One thing, though. These phones will cost you $1000 each." You say, "No problem, Tom. They'll change my life."

In this example, the cell phone has every characteristic working for it. It's *advantageous* over the old land-based phones, especially for someone like Rose. It's *simple* to understand and use; it's *compatible* with the old phones; it's so *adaptable* that you can use it anywhere, anytime; and it enhances your *social connectivity*. What a wonderful new technology!

But, consider Friedman's offer of another change.

So a year later I come back and say, "Charlie, remember that phone I sold you that worked out so well. Well, I've got another deal for you. You see that light up there. I'm going to power that light with solar energy. One thing, though. It'll cost you $100 a month."

You say, "Ah...Ah...Tom, remember that cell phone you sold me—that changed my life. In case you haven't noticed, I already have a light bulb. It works just fine, and I really don't care where the electrons come from."

Four of the change characteristics—*simplicity, compatibility, adaptability,* and *social impact* are neutral. But, the fifth characteristic—*relative advantage*—gets a low, low rating. It costs a lot more and adds no new functionality.

Why should Charlie spend more money to get something he already has? He won't buy into solar light unless it has an advantage over his current light.

Then Friedman makes his point:

Now you see how policy can make the difference. If the government comes in and says, "Charlie, from now on, you're going to have to pay for the CO_2 that light emits and for the cost of the troops in the Persian Gulf to power that light. From here on, that light is going to cost you $110."

Now, when I come along and say, "Charlie, I've got a solar light that will cost you just $100 a month," you say, "Tom, I'll take ten of your solar lights."

In this case, public policy reverses the *relative advantage* of the change, making it adoptable.

How do they compare?

EXERCISE   Now try your skill at rating a couple of organizational changes. You can refer to the Change Aid on the next page. (Change Aids are guides to action and you will find them throughout the book. They are also available free to download at chocochange.com.) After you rate the two changes, you'll find Suggested Answers on the following pages, as well as another Change Aid for optimizing a change.

Change Characteristics from the Adopter's Viewpoint

Relative Advantage To the potential user/adopter, is the change better than alternatives? A change which has relative advantage is better than the alternatives—new or old. This may seem obvious, but it is often overlooked. Even when a change is good for people, they may not notice without help. Valued attributes must be made apparent. This change characteristic is especially important in the early stages of user acceptance when powerful, first perceptions are made.

Simplicity For the potential user/adopter, is the change easy to understand? The simpler a change is to understand, the more acceptable it will be to users.

Adaptability Can potential users/adopters adapt the change for themselves or their jobs? Because most people like what they create themselves, this change characteristic can offset the "not invented here" problem, which is especially prevalent with imposed change. Effective change agents accept and even encourage modifications which don't destroy the critical functions or integrity of the change.

Compatibility Is the change like what users/adopters are used to? A change which has compatibility is one which is similar to that which the person is already used to. The more easily the new system slips into the old one, the better. The change agent looks for ways in which the new is like the old—in tasks to be performed, work patterns, outputs, worker relations, etc.—and then communicates and builds on these similarities.

Social Impact Will users/adopters lose cared-for colleagues or have to deal with unwanted new people? Users tend to value changes that have little or no impact on their relationships with other people, particularly with people they've worked well with. Effective change agents identify ways the change is likely to impact on the existent social system—during training, start-up, or use. Then they plan ways to lessen the impact of any negatively perceived changes and, when positives exist, to emphasize these potentials.

EXERCISE   Read the case and rate the change from 1-5 *from the perspective of the indicated adopters.* Be sure you have a rationale for each of your ratings. Total your ratings.

CASE   An Ohio manufacturing plant had a number of geological engineers who worked in the field. They arranged their own schedules and came and went as they saw fit. One day, the top brass in the company decided that they needed more accountability regarding these engineers. Timeclocks were installed at the sites where the engineers worked and memos were sent out telling the engineers to punch in and out every time they came and went.

The Change: Timeclocks

The Adopters: Geological Field Engineers

	Hard to Implement		**Easy to Implement**
RELATIVE ADVANTAGE	Much worse than alternatives	1 2 3 4 5	Much better than alternatives
SIMPLICITY	Very hard to understand	1 2 3 4 5	Very easy to understand
COMPATIBILITY	Very different from what's usual	1 2 3 4 5	Very similar to what's usual
ADAPTABILITY	Very hard to modify	1 2 3 4 5	Very easy to modify
SOCIAL IMPACT	Very negative re relationships	1 2 3 4 5	Very positive re relationships

TOTAL [   ]

If your total is…

    …20 or above, implementation should be readily do-able.

    …between 10 and 20, implementation will take careful planning.

    …below 10, implementation may be very difficult.

Suggested Answers

Here are suggested answers with rationales. You may disagree somewhat but if you do, be sure you can say why. It's not important to rate everything the way I do, but it is important to have a reason for your rating.

EXERCISE   Geological Engineers & Timeclocks

Relative Advantage 1   These engineers have been an independent group who see absolutely no advantage in having to punch into a timeclock. In fact, they are likely to view it as only slowing them down.

Simplicity 5   It is obviously easy for the engineers to understand how a timeclock works.

Compatibility 1   As said above, these engineers are an independent group and punching into a timeclock is completely counter to the way they've worked all these years.

Adaptability 1   Timeclocks aren't adaptable. You punch in or you don't.

Social Impact 2 or 3   Their educational status, their value to the company, and their free-wheeling behavior have made the engineers an elite group within the organization. To have to punch into a timeclock will be viewed by them as unprofessional and a threat to their social status within the organization.

TOTAL: 10-11   With a total of 10-11, implementation of the timeclocks should be very difficult.

This case is based on a real-world situation. Getting these adopters to make the change was difficult. In fact, it was impossible! Timeclocks were installed and all kinds of accidents happened to them. They were filled with dirt, chewing gum, and other substances. Some months after installation, at one location they were filled with cement. At that, management gave up and removed the timeclocks.

EXERCISE   Read the case and rate the change from 1-5 *from the perspective of the indicated adopters.* Be sure you have a rationale for each of your ratings. Total your ratings.

CASE Department heads at Trextel, a large multinational corporation, have always had free choice of vendors for the purchases of material and services. This means that they can buy from anyone they want to. Often they become friends with vendors and enjoy sporting events and other joint activities. Management has announced a new procedure— to begin in three months—that allows only a select list of approved vendors to be used. There is an appeals procedure but the criteria are very strict.

The Change: New purchasing procedures

The Adopters: Department heads

	<u>Hard to Implement</u>		<u>Easy to Implement</u>
RELATIVE ADVANTAGE	Much worse than alternatives	1 2 3 4 5	Much better than alternatives
SIMPLICITY	Very hard to understand	1 2 3 4 5	Very easy to understand
COMPATIBILITY	Very different from what's usual	1 2 3 4 5	Very similar to what's usual
ADAPTABILITY	Very hard to modify	1 2 3 4 5	Very easy to modify
SOCIAL IMPACT	Very negative re relationships	1 2 3 4 5	Very positive re relationships

TOTAL

If your total is…

   …20 or above, implementation should be readily do-able.

   …between 10 and 20, implementation will take careful planning.

   …below 10, implementation may be very difficult.

Suggested Answers

EXERCISE Department Heads & New Purchasing Procedures

Relative Advantage 2   The argument has been made that the new procedures will save money for the company. Since, as a result of stock options, most of the department heads hold stock in the company, they favor a reduction in overall costs. Even so, the new procedures are going to disrupt their vendor relations. Also, the department heads resent not being trusted.

Simplicity 4   Since they will get a list of acceptable vendors, it is fairly easy for the department heads to understand how the new purchasing procedures work. It won't be so easy to deal with the vendors who don't make the cut.

Compatibility 1   The new procedures are certainly different from the ones the department heads have used all these years.

Adaptability 2   With the new procedures, department heads will be expected to buy only from vendors on the list. Although there is an appeals process to challenge the omission of a vendor, the criteria are very strict.

Social Impact 1 or 2   If their favorite vendors are not on the list, not only will the department heads no longer get invitations to sporting events, but they may lose friends.

TOTAL: 10-11   With a total of 10-11, implementation of the new system for choosing vendors should be very difficult.

This case is also based on a real-world situation. Although the total rating is the same as the first case and the adopters were not happy about the change, the new procedures were adopted. As we will see later, although user perceptions are important, they are not the only factors involved in the successful adoption of a change. In this case, the organizational factor of strong sponsorship at the highest level was the deciding factor.

How to Optimize a Change

Relative Advantage
- ✓ Highlight any real advantages for the users
- ✓ Emphasize aspects which provide quick or high payoff
- ✓ Have cost-effectiveness figures
- ✓ Be ready to acknowledge disadvantages
- ✓ For each disadvantage, offer a compensatory advantage
- ✓ Empathize

Simplicity
- ✓ Prepare a simply worded, comprehensive description of the change
- ✓ Make the change visible via success stories, site visits, testimonials
- ✓ Be ready to acknowledge complexities
- ✓ Relate complexities to training or job aids available
- ✓ Empathize

Compatibility
- ✓ Identify aspects/procedures similar to the way things are done now
- ✓ Build on similarities
- ✓ Be ready to acknowledge dissimilarities
- ✓ Empathize

Adaptability
- ✓ Know aspects users want to modify even if not possible
- ✓ Know aspects that are modifiable without loss of function
- ✓ Be ready to acknowledge lack of adaptability
- ✓ Counter with compensatory advantages
- ✓ Empathize

Social Impact
- ✓ Know what relationships exist among key people and key groups
- ✓ Project how the change will impact on these relationships
- ✓ Be ready to acknowledge potentially stressful social changes
- ✓ Identify and communicate workable alternatives
- ✓ Empathize

Divisibility

One more important characteristic of the change is *divisibility*. It may not matter to the adopter, but it can offer advantages to the change agent.

Divisibility-by-Part   This means that part of the total change can be implemented first. For example, in a residential recycling project, during the first year only newspapers and other paper might be recycled. Once that habit is established, the following year glass and plastic might be added. Or a corporation with a new comprehensive benefits program might introduce one feature, such as daycare, and later introduce other features. In effect, you may begin by breaking the black box into more acceptable parts.

Divisibility-by-Site   This means that while the whole change may need to be implemented at one time, it can first be implemented at a single site. In turn, this site can become a demonstration for later sites. For example, one of five departments might introduce flextime.

If You Want to Read More

From time to time, I'll suggest related readings you might enjoy if you have time. For the topic of change characteristics, you can read more in Rogers' *Diffusion of Innovations*, Chapter 6 "Attributes of Innovations and Their Rate of Adoption." You'll find good stories too.

WORKSHEET 3 Now rate your change *from the adopters' point of view.*

	Hard to Implement		**Easy to Implement**
RELATIVE ADVANTAGE	Much worse than alternatives	1 2 3 4 5	Much better than alternatives
SIMPLICITY	Very hard to understand	1 2 3 4 5	Very easy to understand
COMPATIBILITY	Very different from what's usual	1 2 3 4 5	Very similar to what's usual
ADAPTABILITY	Very hard to modify	1 2 3 4 5	Very easy to modify
SOCIAL IMPACT	Very negative re relationships	1 2 3 4 5	Very positive re relationships

TOTAL [   ]

If your total is…

   …20 or above, implementation should be readily do-able.

   …between 10 and 20, implementation will take careful planning.

   …below 10, implementation may be very difficult.

"You really oughta wanna"

When Bob Mager made this phrase popular in his best-selling book on analyzing performance problems, he wasn't writing about getting people to accept a change, but he could have been. People don't welcome a change just because you think they should.

3. Why People Resist

As you saw in the last chapter, one reason people resist change is because of the characteristics of the change itself. But there are other reasons why people resist making the journey toward a change.

One reason they resist is because of their attachment to the old known way. They're comfortable with things the way they are. It may be their job, their boss, their workplace friends, software they know, their window with a view or a nearby jogging path. Whatever it is, they're used to it. Then somebody comes along and tells them they have to give it up. They have to accept the *loss* of the way things were. Just like that family had to do after the tornado.

Loss The best known theory of loss is that of Elizabeth Kubler-Ross. She proposed five stages of grief to explain how people respond to such catastrophic losses as terminal illness or the death of a loved one.

The Five Stages of Grief

1. **Denial** *This can't be happening*

2. **Anger** *Why me? It's not fair.*

3. **Bargaining** *Maybe I can talk them out of it.*

4. **Depression** *I don't care what happens.*

5. **Acceptance** *Okay, I can deal with this.*

These stages have also been useful in explaining how people react to much lesser losses than those about which Kubler-Ross wrote. People faced with an organizational change may not go through all of the stages or go through them in this order (in fact, some researchers propose that there are no grief stages), but the overall concept can help change agents understand better what's going on with adopters.

When you understand, you're not only better able to facilitate the adopters' progress, but you're better able to accept their negative reactions without taking them personally.

Even When the Change Is Wanted

It's interesting and important to realize that, *even when a person wants the change*, loss is involved. One dramatic example of this is seen with returning war prisoners who sometimes report that they actually miss their captors. Another example comes from Dana Jennings, a recovering cancer patient, who had a similar reaction. The following is based on his report.

I Just Want to Get Out of Here—Or Do I?

Jennings was diagnosed with prostate cancer. He had surgery, hormone therapy, and radiation.

During the two months of radiation treatments, he got used to the treatment procedures—the check-in, the hospital bracelet, the drafty gown, the wait with fellow patients. He learned the names and became friendly with the doctors, nurses, and therapists, and also with the parking attendants and receptionists. He said "It began to feel as familiar as a job."

Then, one day, it was over, and, although he was glad to be done with the radiation, he experienced a letdown he had never expected. "It felt like getting fired or laid off."

No matter what the change is, some loss is involved.

The Bridge Image

The social psychologist, Kurt Lewin, proposed that, normally, people exist in a state of *equilibrium*. But when a change—organizational or otherwise—enters the picture, that equilibrium is upset. Then, people are faced with the need to let go of the way things have been and to move on toward the future. A useful image of that journey is a bridge, because a bridge not only illustrates movement from the way things were to the way things will be, it also suggests that the middle part of the trip may be the scariest.

Lewin also proposed that the journey could be described as involving three stages—*unfreezing, transitioning,* and *refreezing.* To get people to move toward a change, first, you have to "unfreeze" them from the way things are currently—the old way. Then you have to get them through the anxiety-producing "transition." Finally, you have to "refreeze" them in the changed situation—the new way.

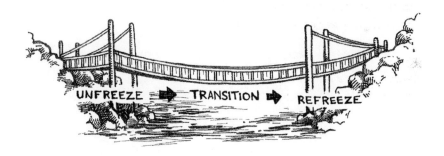

UNFREEZE ➡ TRANSITION ➡ REFREEZE

Edgar Schein, one of the earliest and most respected organizational development experts, had this to say about Lewin's 3-stage concept:

> *I found Lewin's basic change model of unfreezing, changing, and refreezing to be a theoretical foundation upon which change theory could be built solidly. The key, of course, was to see that human change, whether at the individual or group level, was a profound psychological dynamic process that involved painful unlearning without loss of ego identity and difficult relearning as one cognitively attempted to restructure one's thoughts, perceptions, feelings, and attitudes.*

Clearly, change can involve some heavy-duty stuff—on both the emotional and the cognitive level. To facilitate adopters' movement through the process, here are some techniques a change agent might use.

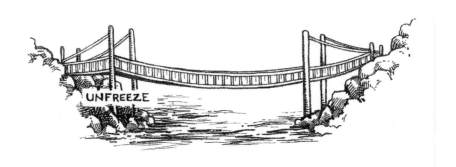

Unfreezing Techniques

Three useful unfreezing techniques are (1) *inform* with valid data about the change, (2) *motivate* with a positive vision of the change, and (3) *modify the environment* to support the change.

Regarding the first two techniques, *information and statistics* may interest people facing a change (especially left-brainers), but *motivation and feelings* are more likely to get them moving (even left-brainers). As John Kotter and Dan Cohen say in *The Heart of Change*, the emphasis should not be on analyze-*think*-change, but on see-*feel*-change.

Chip and Dan Heath in *Switch: How to Change Things When Change is Hard* organize their entire book around a related analogy.

> *…our emotional side is an Elephant and our rational side is its Rider. Perched atop the Elephant, the Rider holds the reins and seems to be the leader. But the Rider's control is precarious because the Rider is so small relative to the Elephant. Anytime the six-ton Elephant and the Rider disagree about which direction to go, the Rider is going to lose. He's completely overmatched.*

To get people to change, you need to activate not only their rational Rider, but their emotional Elephant.

Doing something that both informs and motivates, something that gets people thinking *and* feeling, need not always be costly or complex. You may accomplish it by being creative as illustrated by Kotter and Cohen in this example from *The Heart of Change* (paraphrased here):

Gloves! Gloves! Gloves!

The CEO of a multi-site manufacturing company was convinced that they had a major purchasing issue. He believed that, if the company had a centralized purchasing policy, they could leverage large-scale purchases and save a billion dollars over five years. Currently, each factory had its own suppliers and negotiated its own prices, and the CEO knew that getting support for the new approach from division presidents would be difficult. Then he had an idea.

He sent one of the summer interns out to survey one item that was bought in all of the factories—gloves. When she came back from her investigation, she reported that the factories bought 424 different kinds of gloves. And the prices varied greatly—even for the same glove.

The CEO invited the division presidents to a meeting in the boardroom. When they arrived, they found a table—not piled with papers as usual—but piled with dozens of pairs of gloves. Each pair was tagged with the price paid for it and the factory from which it came.

At first, the presidents were just surprised at the quantity. "We buy all these different kinds of gloves?"

They began to look for gloves from their own factories. It was then that they realized that even when gloves were exactly alike, they varied greatly in price. For example, one glove cost $3.22 when bought at one factory and $10.55 when bought at another.

This activity by the CEO *shook* the division presidents out of their earlier position. After that, the mandate for the change in purchasing policy no longer had to come from the CEO, it came directly from the newly *informed* and *motivated* division presidents. That's creative unfreezing!

Transitioning Techniques

Even after the person has decided to let go of the old way, the first step into the transition can be especially anxiety-producing.

The first step (as well as all the others) can be scary—

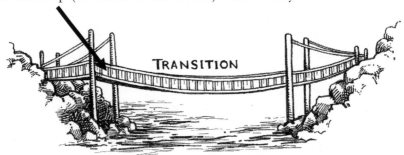

This is a good time for coaching, listening, accepting concerns, and encouraging. When possible, breaking the change down into small steps can also offset anxiety. Other useful techniques include assigning people a meaningful role in the change process and/or involving them in the planning team. Another technique is to redesign the job or work environment so that they cannot perform the job in the old way.

One woman wrote this about transitions:

> *Just realizing there's a word for this experience is quite freeing. I ran into this word used this way once before, when my daughter started Montessori as a three-year old. The main teacher...told me that my daughter had trouble with transitions: going from home or the car to school. So they made a little place for her to go to whenever I dropped her off. She could put her rug in a spot out of the way behind where the work and children were and go lie there or sit and observe or sleep or whatever she wanted to do until she was ready to join the group. She used it perhaps the first week or so and then was fine about going right in after that.*

This story exemplifies some of the techniques suggested for helping a person through an anxiety-producing transition—e.g., listening and accepting concerns, planning small steps. Sometimes, we all need a few baby steps to get going with our transition.

Refreezing Techniques

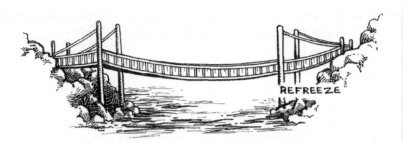

One of the most effective refreezing techniques is that of burning the bridge. If there's no way back, people have little choice but to stay with the change.

Here We Come—Ready or Not

Some years ago I was consulting at a large pharmaceutical company when the order came down that Macs were to be replaced by PCs. The greatest resistance came from the departments with heavy graphics use. However, the order was irrevocable, and the change was scheduled in two stages. At the end of Stage One, Mac support would no longer be made available. At the end of Stage Two, all Macs would be removed from the premises.

After the grumbling was over, people adjusted slowly to the inevitable and—at the end of Stage Two—no Mac users remained (at least not at work). Since the burn-the-bridge technique is likely to be somewhat painful, it's important that the change agent use positive techniques also.

Two such techniques are feedback and rewards. Effective change agents give people feedback on their new performance and on their contribution to the organization, even staging formal rituals to confirm the change and the adopters' part in it. The effective change agent also arranges to get rewards for them—even if it's just a "thanks" from the boss, recognition in a departmental meeting or the company newsletter, or a reserved parking place for a month.

The following Change Aid lists change agent techniques for each of Lewin's three stages.

Techniques for Lewin's 3 Stages

Unfreezing

- Communicate an enticing vision
- Inspire adopters to embrace the change
- Offer data in support of the change
- Set the platform on fire
- Shake them out of the current situation
- Redesign the job or organization

Transitioning

- Encourage adopters to keep moving
- Coach them in the change
- Assign them meaningful roles
- Involve them in planning
- Plan small steps
- Redesign the job or organization

Refreezing

- Burn the bridge
- Provide feedback on performance
- Provide recognition for changing
- Provide rewards for changing
- Stage formal rituals

Change Overload

Throughout the change process, the anxieties and behaviors of the potential adopters may be radically and negatively affected by too many changes. Referring to the effect of such overload, one online site says of the refreezing stage,

> *In modern organizations, this stage is often rather tentative as the next change may well be around the next corner. What is often encouraged, then, is more of a state of 'slushiness' where freezing is never really achieved (theoretically making the next unfreezing easier). The danger with this that many organizations have found is that people fall into a state of change shock, where they work at a low level of efficiency and effectiveness as they await the next change. 'It's not worth it' is a common phrase when asked to improve what they do.*

In a *Harvard Business Review* article, Eric Abrahamson offers a simple acronym for change overload—BOHICA.

Bend-Over-Here-It-Comes-Again!

When your adopters are overloaded, perhaps the best thing you can do is to acknowledge their situation and offer stress-reduction support (more on this in the last chapter).

Exercise The following exercise offers another view of the overload factor. Follow the instructions. Don't read ahead. When you've completed the exercise, go to the following page for a discussion of the results.

EXERCISE Answer before looking ahead.

1. Think of someone you know pretty well—yourself or someone else.

2. CHECK items occurring in the past 6 or so months to the person.

3. List POINTS for each item you checked.

4. Add points to get the TOTAL.

	CHECK	POINTS	
Spouse's death	_____	_____	100
Divorce	_____	_____	75
Close relative's death	_____	_____	65
Injury or illness	_____	_____	55
Marriage	_____	_____	50
Family injury or illness	_____	_____	45
New baby	_____	_____	40
Business readjustment	_____	_____	40
Financial change	_____	_____	40
New line of work	_____	_____	35
More/fewer spouse arguments	_____	_____	35
New mortgage/loan	_____	_____	30
New work responsibilities	_____	_____	30
Son/daughter leaving home	_____	_____	30
Outstanding achievement	_____	_____	30
Spouse begins/stops work	_____	_____	30
New work hours/conditions	_____	_____	20

TOTAL

Another Reason to Resist—Health

Two doctors developed the stress test from which this exercise is adapted. First, they established that, over a two year period, the average American had a 1-in-5 (or 20%) chance of requiring hospitalization. Then, by correlating the scores on their test with subsequent major health problems and hospital admissions, they found the following:

SCORE	MAJOR HEALTH PROBLEM
Under 150	1 in 3 (33%) chance
150 to 300	1 in 2 (50%) chance
Over 300	9 in 10 (90%) chance

As the score goes up, so too does the person's chance of having a major health problem. But, for our purposes, look at just four of these items, items you might check for a person who's having to make a major work change.

Business readjustment	40
New line of work	40
New work responsibilities	30
New work hours/conditions	<u>20</u>
	130

Since people always have more going on in their lives than just your change, it's easy to see that what you're introducing into their lives may push them over the line into a major health problem. So even if they're unaware of it, adopters might resist for another reason—to stay healthy. (Note: This data is from research done over thirty years ago; the results you got should not be taken too seriously. I just wanted to make a point—*People resist when they're stressed and with good reason!*)

Hassle Factors

So far we haven't even factored in the day-in, day-out "hassle factors" that thrust change into our lives.

- ❖ traffic jam on way to work
- ❖ misplaced luggage
- ❖ computer breakdown, lost files
- ❖ coffee spilled on shirt/blouse
- ❖ airline delay
- ❖ billing error
- ❖ rude salesperson
- ❖ tree falls on your house
- ❖ bad weather
- ❖ drop in your child's report card
- ❖ fender bender
- ❖ your dog bites a neighbor

Some psychologists think that hassle factors like these may be even more important in causing health problems than the more impressive sounding items on the earlier stress test list.

You know the expression—"the straw that broke the camel's back."

Change is tough and when several of them pile up—even though some may be trivial— it's even tougher. Regardless of individual styles and personalities, everyone has an overload button. Too much change is just too much!

Adopter Concerns

The *concerns* of adopters have been mentioned several times. A group of researchers at the University of Texas even labeled their model the Concerns-Based Adoption Model (CBAM). Like others, their model involves developmental stages, but it adds a useful description of the kinds of concerns adopters have as they move toward a change.

According to CBAM, once adopters are aware of the change, their concerns evolve from self-concern (lots of "I's" and "me's" in their comments) to concerns about the task/job (mention of the tasks and job) and, finally, to concerns about others and the larger world (comments about customers, clients, the organization, the environment, even the world).

SELF →

TASK →

OTHER

Note that this is exactly the opposite approach from that taken by many—especially high-level managers—who introduce organizational changes to targeted users. First, they present the organizational advantages, next the how-to-do-it activities and eventually they may (or may not) deal with the user's personal concerns.

In sum, people resist change—or accept it—for many reasons, but those reasons almost always begin with the personal. In *Discontinuous Change*, David Nadler and his colleagues explain it this way,

> *When a broad and significant change occurs in the organization, the first question many people ask is "What's in it for me?" or "What's going to happen to me?" These are an indication of the anxiety that occurs when people are faced with the uncertainty associated with organizational change.*

Following the next Change Aid, you have another analysis regarding your own Change Project.

Some Reasons Why...

People Resist Change	People Accept Change

Self
*"I don't get it. I don't like it. I don't like you."**

    less security
    less money
    less opportunity
    less challenge
    less status
    less autonomy
    less authority
    lost contact with liked people
    don't understand it
    don't respect sponsors
    dislike way change presented

Self
"I get it. I like it. I like you."

    more security
    more money
    more opportunity
    more challenge
    more status
    more autonomy
    more authority
    contact with liked people
    do understand it
    respect sponsors
    like way change presented

Task/Job
job harder to do right
poor work arrangement
increases workload
adds confusion
bad timing

Task/Job
job easier to do right
better work arrangement
reduces workload
simplifies
time for a change

Org/Society/World
others will suffer
decreases productivity
decreases profitability
decreases competitiveness
decreases service capacity
bad for organization
bad for society/world

Org/Society/World
others will benefit
increases productivity
increases profitability
increases competitiveness
increases service capacity
good for organization
good for society/world

---

* From Rich Maurer who wrote *Beyond the Wall of Resistance*.

WORKSHEET 4 Get in your adopters' shoes. See the change from *their* viewpoint.

On the left, list every reason—large or small—why your adopters might resist the change. Then, on the right, list all of the reasons they might accept it. Put a star before the 2 or 3 most important reasons for resisting and the 2 or 3 most important reasons for accepting.

REASONS TO RESIST	REASONS TO ACCEPT

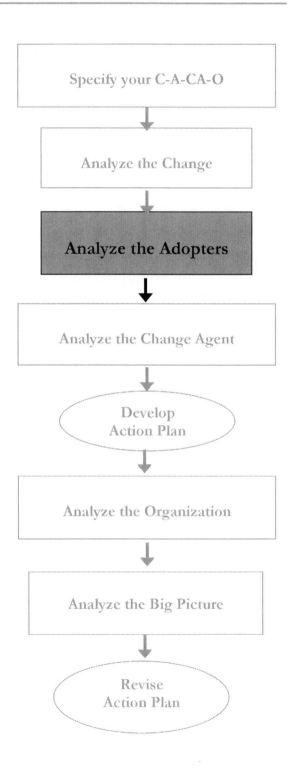

4. The ADOPTERS

Earlier we looked at the change and at why people might resist it. Now we're going to look at the adopters—the people targeted to accept the change.

First, why call them adopters? It is no accident that "adopter" is the most common term used in the change literature. It emphasizes the *dynamic relationship* between the person and the change, as well as the *choice* aspect of the situation.

An Adoption Story

For five years, Mary and John Smith tried to get pregnant. Then, one day their doctor suggested adoption and gave them some literature.

For the next six months, each of them thought about the pro's and con's of adoption. Can I love a baby I didn't create? How will I feel if the baby turns out to have serious health problems? What will my parents think? They went online. They went to the library. Some writers raved about the wonders of parenthood, but others wrote about the pressure they felt from in-laws and friends who made negative comments.

Mary and John began to imagine how their lives would be changed. Long Sunday mornings in bed with the paper and scuba diving vacations would have to go. The guest bedroom would become a nursery.

They decided to check out a local support group. There, they heard from people who had adopted already and from others who were considering adoption. They visited in the homes of several couples with adopted babies and even babysat for some. Finally, they applied at an adoption agency and, six months later, they brought home twins and found that, with all the usual problems of having a baby (well, two babies!), they were thoroughly enjoying their new family.

Adopter Stages

Although they weren't aware of it, Mary and John approached the change they were facing in stages. At the beginning, they hadn't even thought of adoption as a way to have a baby. Then, they got the suggestion and some literature from their doctor. Over time, their attitude and interest in adoption evolved. Facing negatives as well as positives, they were sometimes conflicted. As they became more active, they searched for information and, finally, made the decision to adopt.

Whether people are dealing with a personal change of this kind or an organizational change, they go through evolving stages before they fully integrate the change into their lives or work.

Different researchers and theorists have developed models to describe the stages of adoption. Although the various models have different details, they have much in common. All suggest that adopter stages are developmental. Most suggest that, when adopters adopt, they move from a passive-to-active relationship with the change as well from internal processing to external behavior. Most models state or imply that the middle stages are the most difficult, and all—by virtue of their very existence—suggest that the stages are relatively predictable. (Note: All of these models can be seen as just a further breakdown of Lewin's three stages.) In sum, all models tend to view the change process as...

- **developmental**
- **passive-to-active**
- **internal-to-external**
- **having difficult middle stages**
- **relatively predictable**

It is the predictability of the stages that gives the change agent an opportunity. If you can identify in which stage your adopters are, you can act more appropriately to facilitate movement toward adoption.

The following Chocolate Model stages map well to Lewin's model, are heavily based on Everett Rogers' work, and were influenced by the Concerns-Based-Adoption-Model (CBAM). However, they were designed to be a *practical* guide for use by mid-level organizational change agents.

The Stages of Adoption

1. Awareness

The potential adopter

…is passive about the change
…has little or no information about the change
…has little or no opinion about the change

2. Curiosity

The potential adopter

…is more active regarding the change
…has personal concerns & opinions
…asks questions about the impact on themselves

3. Mental Tryout

The potential adopter

…imagines how it will be with the change made
…has job-focused concerns
…asks questions about task & job impact

4. Hands-on Tryout

The potential adopter

…is ready to learn how to use the change
…has opinions about the change & its use
…asks questions re organization & other impact

5. Adoption

The adopter

…uses the change on the job
…makes suggestions for improvements
…asks detailed questions & may need help

The following is an example of my own adoption of a change.

How I Bought Into a New Technology

In 2005, the Chair of Indiana University's Instructional Systems Technology Department asked me if I would like to teach online. I responded immediately—"Thanks, but there's no way my courses could be put online. They're far too dependent on the human interactive dimension."

A year or so later, Tony Marker, a friend and professor in Instructional and Performance Technology at Boise State University, asked if I'd be interested in teaching change management for them. I repeated my earlier statement, adding that, as a form of learner analysis, in some of my graduate courses I'd even begun to meet with students before class began. Tony said, "You know, it would be your class so, if you wanted to, you could use the first week for telephone interviews." That sounded interesting.

In the months that followed, I began to read articles on online teaching, I searched the web for relevant posts and, over lunch, I interviewed an IU friend who teaches online.

Then in the fall of 2007, I followed along with one of Tony's online courses. I read his students' posted bios and felt like I'd gotten a sense of where they were coming from and what they wanted out of the course. I imagined relating to students though their posted words. I imagined writing my own words to them in e-lectures and comments. Maybe we could interact after all.

In the spring of 2008, I went through Boise State's basic training for online students and faculty and began to cope with the technology.

It had taken three years, but I had moved from "never" to "maybe" to "okay, I'll do it." I designed the 10-week course and developed e-lectures for each week. My first online class was for BSU in the summer of 2008. Since then, I've taught other online courses at BSU and IU and—surprise!—I love teaching online.

If you apply the Chocolate Model's stages of adoption to analyze this change situation—

AWARENESS *In 2005, the Chair of Indiana University's Instructional Systems Technology Department asked me if I would like to teach online. I responded immediately—"Thanks, but there's no way my courses could be put online. They're far too dependent on the human interactive dimension."*

A year or so later, Tony Marker, a friend and professor in Instructional and Performance Technology at Boise State University, asked me if I'd be interested in teaching change management for them. I repeated my earlier statement, adding that, as a form of learner analysis, in some of my graduate courses I'd even begun to meet with students before class began. Tony said, "You know, it would be your class so, if you wanted to, you could use the first week for telephone interviews." That sounded interesting.

CURIOSITY *In the months that followed, I began to read articles on online teaching, I searched the web for relevant posts and, over lunch, I interviewed an IU friend who teaches online.*

MENTAL TRYOUT *Then in the fall of 2007, I followed along with one of Tony's online courses. I read his students' posted bios and felt like I'd gotten a sense of where they were coming from and what they wanted out of the course. I imagined relating to students though their posted words. I imagined writing my own words to them in e-lectures and comments. Maybe we could interact after all.*

HANDS-ON TRYOUT *In the spring of 2008, I went through Boise State's basic training for online students and faculty and began to cope with the online technology.*

ADOPTION *It had taken three years, but I had moved from "never" to "maybe" to "okay, I'll do it." I designed the 10-week course and developed e-lectures for each week. I was better prepared for class than I had ever been. My first online class was for BSU in the summer of 2008. Since then, I've taught other online courses at BSU and IU and—surprise!—I love teaching online.*

This example may cause you to say, "That's about an individual change. That's different from an organizational change." Not really. Adopters may exist in a group, but they adopt individually. It's just practical with organizational changes to plan for them as a group. What follows is an example (based on a real case) of how a group of people go through the adopter stages when they are presented with a change.

Trektel's New Purchasing Processes

For many years, organizations looked mostly at how to make more money. In the late 90's, they also began to look at how to spend less money. This resulted in a lot of companies taking a hard look at their purchasing operation, and adopting new, cost-cutting processes— consolidation, supplier selection, competitive negotiation, and so forth.

The Organization, the Change, & the Adopters *Trektel is a multinational company with over 40,000 employees. The Corporate Purchasing Management Team decided to implement some radically different purchasing processes throughout the company. The change would affect purchasing people at various global sites.*

The CHANGE   = new purchasing processes

The ADOPTERS = 150 purchasing people at various global sites

Stage 1 Awareness The first step for potential adopters involves becoming aware of the change. In this initial stage, they lack information. They are mostly passive and, although they may be receptive to information if it's offered, they neither seek nor avoid information about the change. All other things being equal, they have little opinion about the change. **IF** they receive information that is more positive than negative, they will remain receptive to additional information and move closer to acceptance and use of the change.

At Trextel, the buyers are one important group of potential adopters. When they first hear that new purchasing processes are in the pipeline—since it will affect them—they pay attention!

Stage 2 Curiosity   Once aware of the change, potential adopters become more active. They become curious. In this stage, adopters have left their passivity behind, and they are actively questioning and looking for answers. They are also self-focused and concerned about how this new process or technology will affect them personally. What new demands will it make? Will their roles change? Will their relationship to the decision-making process change? Will reward systems change? **IF** adopters' self-concerns are adequately met during this stage, they may pass willingly to the next stage.

At Trektel, the buyers are beginning to ask—What are these new purchasing processes anyway? Are they going to mess up my relationship with my vendors? I play golf every week with my biggest vendor. What am I going to say if he loses our account? Is this going to mean a lot of over-time? Is my job in jeopardy?

Stage 3 Mental Tryout   Having learned more about the proposed change, potential adopters begin to try it out mentally, to think about how it will work on-the-job. In this stage, adopters imagine the fit between the work they have to do and the new process. Also, they are now able to look beyond their personal concerns and have concerns about job-related issues. They have questions about the impact of the new process on the work itself in terms of scheduling, efficiency, time-demands, management, cost. **IF** they judge the change to be feasible in their own circumstances, they may move willingly to the next stage.

By now Trektel's buyers have gotten quite a bit of information about the new processes and, as they go about their workdays, they think about what a given task would be like if the new system were in place.

Stage 4 Hands-on Tryout   Having decided that they may be able to cope with the change, potential adopters are ready to test it in a real or simulated work situation. Dependent on the nature of the change, this may be a lengthy process. Now adopters have opinions about the new process, are ready to learn how-to, and have questions extending out to departmental, organizational, even community impact. **IF** they feel comfortable about using the change, they may move willingly toward complete acceptance and full use.

Trektel's buyers have attended training workshops and are learning how to use the new processes under conditions like the ones in their own work situation. Although they would rather continue the way things were, they do see that the new approach will save the company millions and perhaps even their jobs. They are already scheduling vendor meetings to explain the new processes.

Stage 5 Adoption   Finally, potential adopters weigh the results of the hands-on tryout and decide to accept and use the change. Their mastery is probably imperfect and they may have some problems with the change on the job. In this stage, adopters have detailed questions and even suggest improvements. **IF** they receive adequate support and reinforcement during this phase, they will probably integrate the change into routine use.

Trektel's buyers find that, once they start using the new processes, problems come up which were never mentioned during training.

Although both of these examples sound as if people proceed from one stage to the next in an orderly fashion, this is not necessarily so. They may regress and go back a stage or loop between stages. They may even appear to skip a stage. Or, they may suddenly balk. The point is that you—as the person trying to guide or facilitate them toward acceptance of a new process or technology—will have more success if you operate from the five-stage basis and prepare for each.

Identifying the Adopter Stage   Once you have an understanding of the stages adopters are likely to go through, you still have to figure out what stage your own adopters are in. For the moment, let's assume you have a lot of data from adopters—statements about their concerns, beliefs, interests in regard to the change. But what does the data—their statements—mean in relation to their stage of adoption?

EXERCISE   Get some practice. On the following page, try to identify an adopter's stage by what s/he says. When you've finished, Suggested Answers follow.

Exercise   In What Stage Is This Adopter?

What adopters say is one clue to what stage they're in. Classify each statement below according to which stage they are likely to be in. You may want to refer to the Change Aid on page 47. Don't look at the next page until after you've answered everything.

> 1 = Awareness
> 2 = Curiosity
> 3 = Mental Tryout
> 4 = Hands-on Tryout
> 5 = Adoption

a. ___ "How will the new method affect the way we work on the assembly line?"

b. ___ "It will work better if you change the valves."

c. ___ "I really don't know anything about it."

d. ___ "I heard that we may get a new supervisor."

e. ___ "A friend of mine over at Compton has been using that software package for a year and he says it's okay.'"

f. ___ "I've got to admit. It's increased sales."

g. ___ "No wonder it works in R & D. They've got resources out their wazoo."

h. ___ "This is just another example of how those guys in the front office can always think of some new way to get us to work harder."

i. ___ "If they'd pay us what they paid that consultant, we could really improve the system."

j.___ "I saw a demonstration but I'm still not so sure it will work in our department.

k. ___ "I think this new software is just going to slow us down when it comes to getting the job done."

l. ___ "As usual, when push comes to shove, it doesn't work the way they said it would."

m. ___ "I can see how it might reduce errors if those techies can just show us how to use it."

Suggested Answers

As with most human behavior, there are often no clear-cut answers. However, you should begin to recognize the difference between someone at an earlier or a later stage of adoption. If your answer is different from those below, justify it according to the descriptions.

> 1 = Awareness
> 2 = Curiosity
> 3 = Mental Tryout
> 4 = Hands-on Tryout
> 5 = Adoption

a. 3 They've moved beyond self-concerns and are now concerned about how the change will affect the job.

b. 5 They've used it and are now suggesting an improvement.

c. 1 They're at ground zero about the change.

d. 1 or 2 They could be barely aware or they could be already worried about working for a new boss. It probably would depend upon how they said it.

e. 3 or 4 Although they don't mention their own work, they do refer to how a friend work is going and what s/he thinks about the change and its use so I give it a 3 or 4.

f. 5 If it's increased sales, they must be using it.

g. 3 This seems to be a job-focused concern—the lack of needed resources.

h. 2 They must be aware since they're complaining, but they don't sound very informed. They do sound concerned about themselves.

i. ? I want to know more before I decide where this fellow is. He could be anywhere from 1-5.

j. 3 or 4 They saw a demonstration so they must know quite a bit about the change, and they're concerned about its impact on the job so I give it a 3. However, they do say "department" so maybe an organizational concern, so then a 4.

k. 3 They express a job-related concern.

l. 5 They must be using it since they say it doesn't work as promised.

m. 4 They seem interested in learning how to use the change.

WORKSHEET 5 Analyze your adopters' stage of adoption.

In your best opinion, in what stage are most of your adopters?
What evidence do you have for making that judgment?
If some adopters vary from the majority's, who are they? What stage do you think they are in? your evidence?

If You Want to Read More

You can read in depth about adopter stages in Rogers' *Diffusion of Innovations*, Chapter 5 "The Innovation-Decision Process." More good stories.

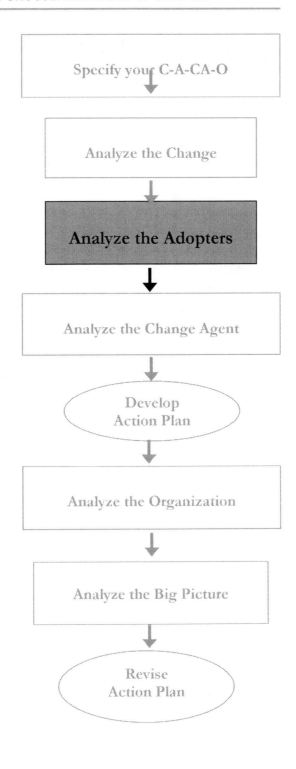

5. The ADOPTER Group

Up to now, we've been looking at the adopters mostly as individuals. Now, we're going to look at them as a group and also at how some key adopters can have an effect on the adoption process.

Opinion Leaders

In just about every ongoing group, there are certain key people to whom others turn for information and guidance. These are *opinion leaders*.

Of course, they vary dependent on what the topic is. For example, in an organizational setting, people might turn to one person for information and guidance about a proposed software system and to another for information and guidance about the way to deal with a new manager.

The question for you as a change agent is—To whom does the group look for information and guidance *about your change?*

Once you've identified the opinion leader(s), you can study them to understand the group better because the person who has come to be regarded as an opinion leader is one who—although perhaps exceptional in competency and know-how—is a lot like the majority of the group members. He or she conforms to the group norms and is at the center of the group's communication network. One change expert, Ronald Havelock, described them this way,

> *Opinion leaders. . . are certain influential people who are held in high esteem by the great majority of their fellow men. . . They watch the innovator to see how the idea works, and they watch the resister to test the social risks of adopting the idea. Indeed, in many cases they are eager to observe these changes because their continuance in power rests upon their ability to judge innovations. They want to be champions of the innovation whose time has come.*

Using Opinion Leaders   Once you have identified the opinion leaders within your adopter group, you should try to enlist their support for your change. However, Havelock's insightful phrase—"champions of the innovation whose time has come"—is also a warning to the change agent. Smart opinion leaders are not going to lose a position of influence within the group just to support a change that they perceive to be a bad idea. Note also that as opinion leaders speak out regarding a change, they may come to be seen by their peers as too much like the change agent and no longer like a fellow worker. In this event, they will have lost credibility. Lastly, because opinion leaders have high potential value, when they are called upon to help too often, they may be "worn out" by change agents. With these caveats in mind, the opinion leader is probably your most important ally in the adopter group and one whose influence you should use with care.

How to Find Opinion Leaders   It's all well and good to know that opinion leaders can be of help in a change project, but how do you know who they are? Obviously, you can ask. But whom do you ask, what do you ask, and can you rely on the answers?

If you are familiar with the adopters, you may already know who the opinion leaders are. All it takes is asking yourself the right question—Who is likely to be an opinion leader *for this change*? But be aware that you may not have a valid view. After all, you're probably not a member of the group.

Another source of information is the group itself. People usually know who their opinion leaders are, so if you have the opportunity, you can ask them. You can be unobtrusive and tuck the question into a broader conversation. But be aware that the focus of your question will make a difference. *Be sure it relates to the change at hand.* For example, if you ask the general question "Whom do you ask for advice?" you may get a different answer from when you ask "Who do you think has the best understanding of what this change will mean on the job?"

As noted above, people follow different opinion leaders depending on what the task is. When the task relates to technology, people may turn to one person, but when the task relates to a procedural or political problem, they may turn to another.

How much can you count on the answers to be accurate? One way is to ask more than one person. In addition to group members, bosses or others outside of the group may be useful sources of information. If several people give you the same answer, you can move ahead with some assurance that you have identified the right person or persons.

The Social System

There's more to be learned about the adopter group than just the names of a few key individuals. The most effective change agent also develops a mental picture of the entire adopter group, seeing it as a *social system.*

According to Rogers,

> *A social system is a set of interrelated units that are engaged in joint problem solving to accomplish a common goal. A system has structure, defined as the patterned arrangements of the units in a system, which gives stability and regularity to individual behavior in a system. The social and communication structure of a system facilitates or impedes the diffusion of innovations in the system.*

Any mention of social systems is likely to remind you of electronic *social networks* such as Facebook. Indeed, they are likely to become increasingly important in the implementation of organizational changes, and, hence, they'll be discussed in a later chapter.

For now, let's look at what change researchers have to say about certain individuals in the adopter group and how they relate. How do they communicate? Who talks to whom? Who asks whom for advice? Who's a leader? Who's an isolate?

This kind of information may be hard to get from the near-anonymity of a national or international virtual group, but it's available in most organizational settings.

A Tool for Understanding   One of the best tools for mapping such group relations is a *sociogram.*

Although all sociograms show relationships among individual members or units in a group (represented by circles), they vary in what they portray, dependent upon what aspect of the relationship is of interest, an interest often expressed as a question. Here's a simple example.

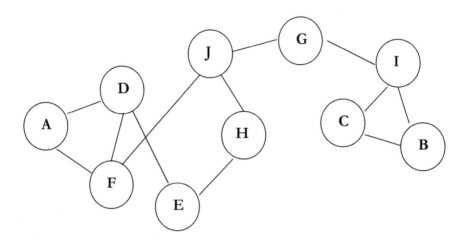

The lines connecting all 10 of the individuals indicate that everyone in the group has some kind of relationship with someone else. But since we don't know what was of interest or what question they were asked, we don't know why they chose the people they did. Were their choices based on friendship, athletic prowess, project work, what?

And since no directionality is shown (the lines have no arrows), we don't know who is choosing whom. For example, did G chose I? or did I choose G? Or did they choose each other? To know which way the choices went, we need arrows.

Even without arrows though, we can see that two possible sub-groups (AFD and CIB) may exist within the larger group.

And, we can also see that one person (G) may be less connected to the group than others are.

Now assume that the question asked of each person is "What two people would you like to work with on this project?" Lines show choices and arrows show who chose whom. So, what do we know from this sociogram?

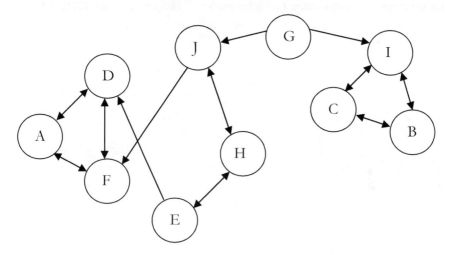

As speculated earlier, there seem to be two subgroups—ADF and CIB—whose members chose each other. However, two members from one group—D and F—also got a vote from outside, suggesting they have connections from outside their group. On the other hand, CIB got only one vote from outside and that one was from G who is a bit of a loner. So, CIB seems to be a sub-group somewhat apart from the larger group.

What about the rest of the members? H and J each got two votes. Hence, while they may be somewhat independent of others, they seem to have some connections within the larger group. What about G? Since G got no votes, G appears to be an isolate, perhaps by choice, through social ineptness, or just newness to the group.

Who is likely to be an *opinion leader?* (Answer before reading further.)

Since D got the most votes (though not significantly more) and belongs to what looks like a mutually supportive sub-group, D may be the most likely candidate for opinion leader. Also E voted for D and has connections with H and J, so these three might follow D's leadership. Similarly, since G voted for J, G might also follow D. The challenge for D (and the change agent as well) might be the CIB sub-group which shows no ties to the larger group.

A word of caution about the G's in the world. Their isolation suggests that they don't communicate or connect well with others in the group. However, the reasons can be varied. As suggested above, it may be personality or different interests or it may just be that they are new to the group. Or they could even be innovators. (More on innovators later.) In any event, their position on the sociogram suggests that you may want to get more information about them. They may require special assistance, but they also may have something of value to offer.

Virtual Groups In both sociograms above, the individuals were members of a face-to-face group. The situation is far more difficult to get information from, and to understand, in an online, virtual group such as those found in change projects that cut across national or international borders and in which communication is never face-to-face. Marshal B. Anderson did a sociogram of an on-line group of 30 or so students and made this comment:

> *Only 12 of the group members are actually shown in this diagram because the rest were isolates… we can identify two possible groupings amongst the members displayed…but these would seem to be of little value as they can not take account of the remaining 18 members…This shows a number of 'stars' emerging…round which groups could undoubtedly form, but there is nothing like the spread of interest we saw in the real world group.*

> *Why might this be? One possible explanation might be that the real world group is much more likely to know each other in a more general sense and to have set up social as well as working relationships.*

Managing communication and influence within an adopter group is always a challenge, but it is even more challenging with an online or virtual group.

Build a mental image! Given organizations today, not to mention political correctness, you may never do a formal sociogram. However, just being able to think about a group this way—and to get a mental image—can be useful in understanding your adopter group.

WORKSHEET 6 Create a sociogram of your adopter group. If at all possible, first do some observations and even careful question-asking. (See Appendix B for instructions on how to make a sociogram.)

Be careful with your questions! If you do gather information directly, be very careful in the way you ask the question—both for its content and for your style. Questions related to personal relations can be touchy and off-putting.

Also, treat the information you get with the greatest confidentiality. Not only because it's the right thing to do, but because if even one adopter decides that you can't be trusted, your effectiveness as a change agent may be seriously reduced. With this in mind, sociograms are probably not parts of the project plan you should post on your cubicle wall.

Consider all results as hypotheses! You may have noticed that in interpreting the above sociograms, I used words like "might be," "seems to be," and "suggests." That's because, with such a once-over-lightly use of the sociogram, all interpretations should be viewed as tentative hypotheses. So long as you don't get locked into the results, though, even a rough sociogram can help.

The Adoption Curve

It's obvious that—within any group—individuals adopt a change at different rates. However, it's not so obvious that there is a predictable pattern to the way a group of people adopt. This pattern has been repeatedly verified by actual data and is illustrated below in Everett Rogers' "bell curve of adoption." The horizontal axis represents *time;* the vertical axis represents the *number of people* who adopt at any given time. (Note that rate-of-adoption is commonly shown in a bell curve; however, it can also be shown in an S-curve. See End Notes.)

At the beginning (left end of the curve), a very few people (2.5 %) are quick to adopt—the *innovators.* Bringing up the rear (right end of the curve), a few people (16%) are very slow to adopt—the *traditionalists**.* Most people are in the middle—the *early adopters, early majority,* and *late majority.*

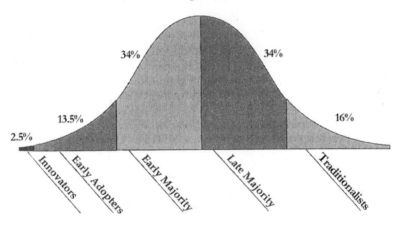

The Adoption Curve

---

* Rogers refers to this last-to-adopt group as "laggards" which even he suggests has an inappropriately negative connotation. Hence, in the Chocolate Model, this group is labeled "traditionalists." Note that any label is really for your understanding and to be used publicly only with caution.

Key Adopters

Among all the people in an adopter group, some are more important than others in your change effort. This is because certain adopters can be key in offering leadership through demonstration of the change or identification of its problems. As noted earlier, the *opinion leaders* are usually the most important for your efforts. However, before looking at them again, let's look at two other potentially key roles—those of *innovator* and of *traditionalist*.

Innovators   Since innovators are the first to adopt, they might seem to be likely demonstrators of the change for others in the adopter group. However, Rogers describes innovators this way:

> *The salient value of the innovator is venturesomeness, due to a desire for the rash, the daring, and the risky. The innovator must also be willing to accept an occasional setback when a new idea proves unsuccessful, as inevitably happens. While an innovator may not be respected by other members of a local system, the innovator plays an important role in the diffusion process: that of launching the new idea in the system...*

Obviously, then, you need to be cautious in enlisting an innovator to help. Why? Because, as Rogers implies, they may be seen as odd-balls, and, hence, their opinions may not impress their peers. For example, unless all members of the group are techies, the group may not be reassured about a new technology just because their techie member says it's great. "After all, Nate lives for the latest electronic gadget. Just because he loves it doesn't mean I will." But if you can identify innovators who are *acceptable* to their peers, they can be very useful, especially when adopters are in the third stage of mental tryout and a demonstration is needed.

Traditionalists   Since traditionalists are the last to adopt, it might seem that they have nothing to offer in a change effort. Their negativity may even be destructive. Rogers describes them this way:

> *The point of reference for the [traditionalist]... is the past. Decisions are often made in terms of what has been done previously...[they] tend to be suspicious of innovations and of change agents.*

At first, you might think that the best way to deal with such folks is to ignore them. However, if you can identify them, you may—just by listening—reduce their need to criticize. Besides, some of their observations may be valid and serve as early warning signals of what's about to go wrong. In that case, you may be able to suggest modifications to the change or to the way it's introduced or, if that's not possible, you can at least be ready for what's to come.

In any event, whether the traditionalists can be brought around or not, it always works out better in the long run if you show respect for all of your adopters, whatever their views and however slow they may be to adopt. Note also that both traditionalists and innovators may show up in a sociogram as isolates—for entirely different reasons.

Opinion Leaders As noted earlier, the most important key people in the adopter group are the opinion leaders. Remember—"They watch the innovator to see how the idea works, and they watch the resister to test the social risks of adopting the idea." In other words, they check out both extremes and, if they decide to adopt, they are usually found *among the early adopters.*

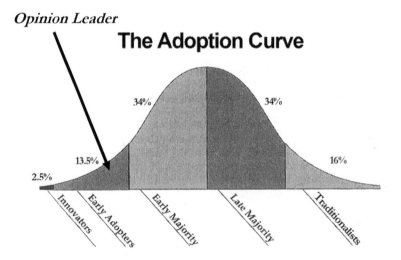

Change Aid The following Change Aid summarizes the characteristics and potential roles of key adopters.

Key Adopters
Characteristics & Roles

Opinion Leaders

➤ Are neither the first nor the last to make a change
➤ Have influence with the adopter group
➤ Represent the norms of the adopter group
➤ Are at the hub of the adopter communications network
➤ Observe innovators to see the pros and cons of the change
➤ Observe traditionalists to learn about the change's limitations
➤ Are relied on by the group for good judgment

Roles: leader, collaborative planner, change spokesperson

Acceptable Innovators

➤ Are among the first to change
➤ Are risk-takers
➤ Are energetic
➤ May or may not have credibility with the group
➤ Are self-confident in areas related to the change
➤ Have information sources outside of the group

Roles: pilot tester, demonstrator

Traditionalists

➤ Are among the last to change
➤ Prefer the status quo
➤ Have opinions about what's wrong with the change
➤ Doubtful of decision-makers and authorities
➤ May or may not have a following in adopter group
➤ Can have a negative impact

Roles: possible problem identifier, naysayer, troublemaker

WORKSHEET 7   Identify the probable key people in your adopter group.

Opinion Leaders	
Innovators	
Traditionalists	

Something Else to Think About

Malcolm Gladwell's highly readable and enjoyable book, *The Tipping Point*, is directly related to the function of a group and its adoption of a change. In fact, the title of Gladwell's book refers to the point on Rogers' adoption curve when momentum takes over—the "word-of-mouth epidemic" that occurs right after the Innovators and the Early Adopters buy in. So, if you can get them aboard, your change is almost certain to be adopted.

Gladwell also describes three roles—different from Rogers' roles—that can facilitate a change: Mavens, Connectors, and Salesmen. He says, "Mavens are data banks…Connectors are social glue…Salesmen [have] the skills to persuade us." You can see that these roles don't map directly onto Rogers' three key roles. However, what they can do is give you an additional tool for finding adopters who may help you.

Of Mavens, Gladwell says,

> *Mavens have the knowledge and the social skills to start word-of-mouth epidemics. What sets Mavens apart, though, is not so much what they know but how they pass it along. The fact that Mavens want to help, for no other reason than because they like to help, turns out to be an awfully effective way of getting someone's attention.*

So Mavens want to be helpers and they have the "knowledge and the social skills" to do so. If you have an "acceptable innovator." you may have found your Maven. However, if not, keep looking. Is there another adopter who fits the description?

Of Connectors, Gladwell says,

> *Connectors are important for more than simply the number of people they know. Their importance is also a function of the kinds of people they know…They are people whom all of us can reach in only a few steps because, for one reason or another, they manage to occupy many different worlds and subcultures and niches…by having a foot in so many different worlds, they have the effect of bringing them all together.*

Think about your adopter group—Is there anyone who connects with different groups—the techies, the people people, the politicians, other sub-groups? She or he may also be an opinion leader, maybe an innovator or one of the majority, but probably not a traditionalist.

Of Salesmen, Gladwell says,

> *…a select group of people—Salesmen—with the skills to persuade us when we are unconvinced of what we are hearing, and they are as critical to the tipping of word-of-mouth epidemics as the other two groups…It's energy. It's enthusiasm. It's charm. It's likeability. It's all those things and yet something more. [It's] optimism.*

If you have a salesman, he or she could be anywhere (although not likely to be among the traditionalists) and might make an exceptional spokesperson for your change at various times in the adoption process.

WORKSHEET 8 Identify probable candidates for Gladwell's three roles. They may or may not overlap Rogers' three key adopter roles.

Connectors	
Mavens	
Salesmen	

If You Want to Read More

By all means, read Malcolm Gladwell's *The Tipping Point*. If your change is a high tech product, you might also find Geoffrey Moore's *Crossing the Chasm* useful. And you can read in depth about the adopter group in Chapter 7 "Innovativeness and Adopter Categories" in Rogers' *Diffusion of Innovations*.

6. DATA GATHERING

Up to now, you've been the source of most of the data. You've answered such questions as—What reasons do *you* think the adopters might have for resisting or accepting your change? Who do *you* think the opinion leaders, acceptable innovators, and traditionalists are? If you haven't done so earlier, it's time to go directly to the adopters and others to check out the accuracy of your opinions. It's time to get first-hand data. But where do you get it? The answer is anywhere and any (legitimate) way you can.

Some ways may be quite informal and much like those upon which you based your earlier answers. They involve observation more than anything else, e.g., in meetings, over lunch, in the elevator. Other ways may be more formal, for example, an interview. But whether you're overhearing comments in the elevator or doing a formal interview, the most important thing you can do is…

LISTEN! LISTEN! LISTEN!

Listening We all tend to take listening for granted. Somebody speaks and we listen. Or do we? A lot of words have been written and a lot of workshops given about listening, especially about *active* listening. But, what is it? Would you know it if you saw it? One good place to practice active listening is during an interview.

EXERCISE At this point, there are two ways you can go. You can stop reading here and go to the Interviewing Exercise in Appendix C. Almost all who do this exercise—even when they're experienced interviewers—are surprised at how much they learn about their own interviewing behaviors. That's the good news. The not-so-good news is that the exercise takes several hours and requires a recorder. What can I say? I think it's worth your time and effort. When you've completed the exercise (or decided not to do it), read on.

A Sample Interview   Following is the transcript of an interview by someone who wants information on why a man bought a hybrid car and on how satisfied he is with his purchase.

Maria: *I heard that you got your car back in 2005. How did you come to buy a hybrid before they became popular?*

Paul: *Oh, I'd been reading about the impact of pollution on the planet.*

Maria: *So you bought because of the environment?*

Paul: *I guess that was the main reason. Of course, I wanted to cut gas consumption.*

Maria: *To save money?*

Paul: *Sure, everybody wants to save money, don't they!*

Maria: *I believe you got one of the first models. Were you concerned about whether they'd gotten all of the design kinks out?*

Paul: *I read everything about the technology and I got online with hybrid owners.*

Maria: *And they reassured you?*

Paul: *Pretty much. Ultimately, I just decided to go for it.*

Maria: *How has it worked out?*

Paul: *I'm fine with it.*

Maria: *What do your friends think?*

Paul: *I think most of them approve.* (He grinned.) *Even if they wouldn't buy one themselves.* (Sounding satisfied with himself.) *Not yet at least.*

Maria: *I get the feeling that you're kind of proud of owning a hybrid.*

Paul (grinning): *You're right. I am. From the beginning, it's made me feel good.*

Maria: *All in all, you seem quite satisfied with your purchase.*

Paul: *Yes, you could say that.*

It's clear from this script that Paul approves of hybrid cars, but what does Maria think about them? The answer is—*You don't know.*

No Opinion! Although Maria spoke as much as Paul did, at no time did she indicate how she felt about hybrid cars. That's one indicator of a good interviewer. At the earliest stage of adoption...

Don't sell* the change!

No Judgment! While Maria may or may not approve of people who buy hybrids, you don't find out here what she thinks about Paul. That's another indicator of a good interviewer. At all stages...

Don't judge the adopter!

Before we further analyze Maria's interview of Paul, let's look at the goal and some techniques of active listening.

---

* By now, you might ask if change agentry is just another name for marketing or selling. Well, there's marketing and there's marketing, and there's selling and there's selling. When engaged in the way Philip Kotler (the most honored marketing professional of all time) or Robert Miller (co-author of *Strategic Selling*) recommend, both marketing and selling are ethical, customer-focused, win-win endeavors. And, yes, then they do have a lot in common with *facilitative change agentry*. With all three, a basic goal is to know the *needs* of the targeted people and provide them with *something of value*. Even so, don't try to *sell* your change too soon in the adoption process.

The Goal and Techniques of Active Listening The goal of active listening is to understand where the other person is coming from.

What is *his/her* view? What does *he/she* think or feel? What is *his/her* opinion? What are *his/her* concerns?

What are they really thinking?

If you are the kind of person who is genuinely interested in other people—a big advantage for a change agent—you probably already use some of the following techniques.

Suggestions for Interviewers

1. Ahead of Time   Plan ahead. List your questions. You may not use all of them or use them in the order you plan, but you'll have them as a reference so you can cover all areas.

2. During the Interview

1. *Focus on what they know, think, and feel* about the potential change. Don't plant ideas or insert your own opinions. (Hard to resist when what you really want to do is persuade them to adopt the change.)

2. *Use open-ended questions* that get people talking. (Avoid questions that can be answered Yes or No.)

3. *Accept without judgment* what the person says. (It's a form of respect and it goes a long way.)

4. *Reflect or mirror* what the person says. This often elicits more information. (Ex. "So if I hear you correctly, you're a bit concerned about how the new system will affect the safety of the workers.")

5. *Ask follow-up questions* to encourage elaboration so you can better understand where the person is coming from. (Ex. "Could you tell me a bit more about that?")

6. *Summarize* the person's main point(s) at the end.

3. At the End   Regardless of what needs you have, an interview involves two people. The most satisfying interviews result in your getting the information you want and the interviewee getting something too—even if it is just a good feeling about the time spent. Thank them for helping you to understand their concerns about the change, possible issues with the change, whatever.

Assuming she planned ahead, let's see how Maria used some of these techniques in her simple interview.

Maria: *I heard that you got your car back in 2005. How did you come to buy a hybrid before they became popular?* OPEN-ENDED QUESTION

Paul: *Oh, I'd been reading about the impact of pollution on the planet.*

Maria: *So you bought because of the environment?* REFLECTION

Paul: *I guess that was the main reason. Of course, I wanted to cut gas consumption.*

Maria: *To save money?* FOLLOW-UP QUESTION (to check out her assumption that money, as well as gas, was one of his motives)

Paul: *Sure, everybody wants to save money, don't they!*

Maria: *I believe you got one of the first models. What were your concerns?* OPEN-ENDED QUESTION

Paul: *I really didn't have any. I'd read a lot about the technology and talked online with other hybrid owners.*

Maria: So you were pretty confident about the car? FOLLOW-UP QUESTION

Paul: *Pretty much. Ultimately, I just decided to go for it.*

Maria: How has it worked out?   OPEN-ENDED QUESTION

Paul: *I'm fine with it.*

Maria: *What do your friends think?* OPEN-ENDED QUESTION

Paul: *I think most of them approve.* (He grinned.) *Even if they wouldn't buy one themselves.* (Sounding satisfied with himself.) *Not yet at least.*

Maria: I *get the feeling that you're kind of proud of owning a hybrid?* FOLLOW-UP QUESTION (asked because of his tone of voice)

Paul (grinning): *You're right. I am. From the beginning, it's made me feel good.*

Maria: *All in all, you seem totally satisfied with your purchase.* SUMMATION

Paul: *Yes, you could say that.*

Other Techniques

Silence   A technique not in the list above is silence. Yet, it can be a powerful tool for getting additional information. While it's important not to cause the other person discomfort with too long a silence, sometimes, after a response, if you wait a bit, the other person will elaborate or add new information voluntarily. And sometimes that information is quite surprising and informative.

Nonverbal Messages   Although nothing in the above transcript suggests that Maria was judging, the fact is she might have been giving non-verbal cues about her opinion of both hybrid cars and their owners. When you interview to learn your adopters' views, it's important not to let your non-verbals send unintended messages. But two non-verbal messages you *should* send are

✓ **INTEREST** *"I'm interested in what you're saying."*

✓ **RESPECT** *"Whatever your views are, I respect you."*

Nonverbal means for expressing interest and respect include your

- eye contact
- tone of voice
- facial expressions
- body position

Trust

Trust is especially important when you are gathering information from people who work in the organization in which you also work or consult. If they tell you the truth about their concerns or about other people, will their words come back to hurt them? Generally, it's wise to treat all data as anonymous so far as others are concerned. If you do offer confidentiality, never, never betray it because, once their trust in you is broken, it is next to impossible to win back.

It's just a Hypothesis! As you gather data on the adopters, consider your early opinions as hypotheses to be revisited as you gather more information. Don't decide with certainty what stage they're in on the basis of one statement or even one interview.

Every Contact Counts! The minute you contact an adopter, your relationship and the implementation of your change have begun. They won't forget!

For Fun (and to become more aware of interviewing techniques)

Watch a PBS Charlie Rose Show and look for examples of poor interviewing techniques. Although Rose attracts an amazing group of interviewees and although he is well-informed on a broad range of subjects, he engages in many poor interviewing behaviors. For example, he *interrupts.* He states a question, indicates through inflection that he is through talking and then, when the person starts to answer, Rose *talks over* them to add more information, give his own answer, or just ask the same question in a different way. He also has many ways of *drawing attention to himself.* Only Presidents, those of great wealth, or those who are terminally ill seem to keep him in line. You can sample recent shows online at the *Charlie Rose Show.*

WORKSHEET 9   Interview your adopters.

1. **Interview at least 3-5 of your adopters** (more if you can). Try to sample innovators, opinion leaders, and traditionalists. If at all possible, interview face-to-face. Next best is the phone. If absolutely necessary, online media will do.

Remember to keep yourself out of the interview. You are there to learn about the adopters' views.

2. **Summarize the results of each interview.** Indicate in which adoption stage you think each interviewee is. Note examples of his/her responses that back up your hypotheses. Writing down what they actually say can help you be more thoughtful about their stage. Also, it will help you communicate with any others who may be working with you. (See Appendix D for an example of one change agent's interview results and method of recording.)

3. Now that you have first-hand information, **revisit your list of reasons for resisting or accepting** (WORKSHEET 4, page 43). Note any changes to your list. Sometimes, people are surprised at the difference between their view and the adopters' actual concerns.

Note: Earlier, you were asked to give your opinions about adopters' concerns and only now are you being asked to go directly to the adopters. There were two reasons for this. One is that you can't learn everything all at once. Another is that doing things in this order may point out the difference between *your* views and *their* views. In general, however, while it's okay to speculate about your adopters' concerns, it's critically important to get first-hand information from them as soon as possible.

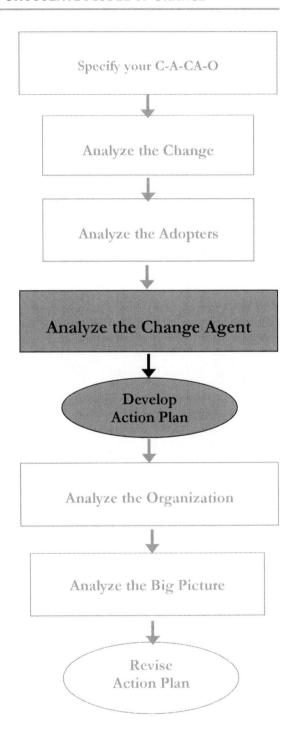

7. The CHANGE AGENT
Strategies & Tactics

In the earlier section on adopters, you learned that people go through relatively predictable stages as they move toward accepting (or not) a change, and you got some experience at applying the stage concept to potential adopters in the real world. Analysis is not enough.

No analysis paralysis here!

As a change agent, what should you DO to help adopters accept and use the change? Just as the stages are different, so too are the related strategies and tactics different.

The Chocolate Model offers strategies and tactics as they relate to each adoption stage. How can you...

> ...make adopters **aware** of the change?

> ...satisfy adopter **curiosity** about the change?

> ...help adopters positively **imagine** the change in action?

> ...help adopters **tryout** the change?

> ...help adopters effectively **use** the change in their work?

Let's look again at the stages of adoption, but now add a strategy for each stage.

For Stage 1 Awareness

When adopters are approaching Stage 1, the way they first hear about the change is important. First impressions are hard to dispel. But it's not enough to be clear and accurate; it's also important not to try for too much or to say too much at this early stage. People don't want a load of information when they barely know anything about the topic. So don't overwhelm them with a big information campaign or training program. And don't try to persuade them either. For now, just offer a vision—a positive view of the other side of the bridge.

When adopters are in **STAGE 1 AWARENESS** passive about the change little/no info about the change little/no opinion about the change		You should **ADVERTISE** get their attention be brief & positive appeal to their needs

This is the time to be an ADVERTISER! The goal is to "jump start" the process of adoption. (Mass media can be useful at this initial stage.) Be brief and positive! And, most of all, appeal to *their* needs and consider *their* concerns. Remember the CEO's gloves!

Let's return to the Trektel example. How might a change agent introduce the new purchasing procedures to global buyers?

> *A well-respected, top-level executive sends a video message to all purchasing buyers worldwide. CREDIBLE SOURCE USING A MASS MEDIA He begins by saying that these are competitive times and anything that saves money also saves jobs. FOCUS ON THEM Then, he says that some new purchasing procedures have brought enormous savings to other companies and are soon to be rolled out at Trektel. He acknowledges that, at the beginning, these new procedures will be a challenge for the buyers. FOCUS ON THEM He expresses his appreciation and the company's need for their help in achieving the goal of significant savings. EFFORT TO INSPIRE He indicates what they can next expect. MEETS THEIR NEED TO KNOW.*

For Stage 2 Curiosity

When adopters are in Stage 2, they are aware of the change and becoming more active. They may look for information, but they are still focused on their own concerns, so this is where—if they don't get good information—they may have needless anxiety and "horribilize" like the boy in the airplane story, or even turn against the change.

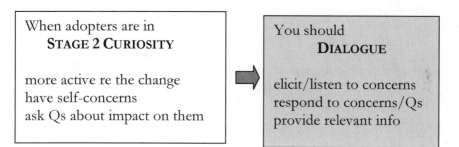

For change agents to offer appropriate information and reassurance, they need to know what the adopters know and also what their concerns and questions are. Listen carefully, provide answers if you can, and be understanding and supportive. Information needs to flow both ways. In short, dialogue.

How might a change agent DIALOGUE with Trektel's purchasing people about the new purchasing procedures?

Now that the adopters (the buyers) have become aware that new purchasing procedures are on the way, we need to know what their reactions are. What are their concerns? The change agent needs ways to exchange information and concerns. He does telephone interviews with a few adopters from each site ELICITS CONCERNS and sets up a column on Purchasing's web page— "Twenty Questions Buyers Are Most Frequently Asking." The change agent's responses to such questions are honest and as informative as possible. RESPONDS TO CONCERNS & PROVIDES RELEVANT INFORMATION "I don't know yet but I'll let you know as soon as I can." Answers often elicit more questions or concerns. The change agent monitors the web site daily and responds frequently.

If you haven't already interviewed representative adopters, as well as technical experts on the change, this is the time to do it. Also, if you can, interview people at some other site who are already using the change. What worked for them? What gave them problems?

When you have this kind of user-based information, you are ready to be a good customer-service person. Only in this case, the adopters are your customers.

For Stage 3 Mental Tryout

When adopters are in Stage 3, they are moving from a focus on themselves to a focus on the task or the job. They imagine the change as it might be in the workplace. They ask, "How does this change really work?" It's time now to give them specific, realistic "good images" to think about.

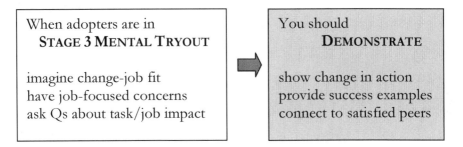

They need credible success stories, case histories, a chance to see the change working. If possible, arrange a site visit to a successful use of the new process, technology, etc.

Be sure the site is as similar as possible to that of the adopters. If your adopters work in a small organization with limited resources and you take them to a giant corporation, they may think, "Oh, sure! It'll work for them. But, what about us? We don't have their resources."

How might a change agent DEMONSTRATE the new purchasing procedures to Trektel's buyers?

At the Annual Global Purchasing Conference which is attended by representative purchasing people from all Trektel sites, a team of purchasing people from a pilot site makes a presentation on the use of the new procedures. (PEER GROUP and mock-DEMONSTRATION)

Team members are some of the best-known and respected buyers in the company. (CREDIBLE SOURCE) Their presentation deals with typical purchases and they discuss both their successful results and the problems encountered along the way and how they dealt with them. Questions are encouraged.

A demonstration is most effective when the presenter is highly credible to the adopters. Credibility is of two kinds: competency and trustworthiness. Demonstrators who have successfully adopted the change are likely to be seen as competent and, if they are also peers—rather than managers, consultants, or change agents who may have selfish motives or manipulative intentions—they are likely to be seen as trustworthy too. An opinion leader or acceptable innovator who has become a user of the change has both kinds of credibility.

For Stage 4 Hands-on Tryout

Now users are no longer asking "How does it work?" Now they are asking "How can I do it myself? How can I use it?" They need the skills and knowledge to use the change effectively. They are ready for hands-on experience, for training and job aids that relate to job performance.

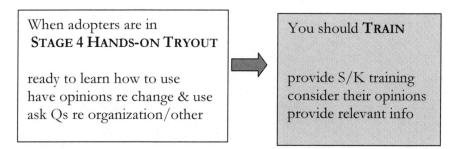

When adopters are in
STAGE 4 HANDS-ON TRYOUT

ready to learn how to use
have opinions re change & use
ask Qs re organization/other

You should **TRAIN**

provide S/K training
consider their opinions
provide relevant info

What might a change agent do to TRAIN Trektel's purchasing people in the new purchasing procedures?

> *Most of the training is supplied in workshops put on by experienced trainers from the external consulting group that designed the new procedures. (PERFORMANCE-ORIENTED TRAINING) They cover such topics as identification of qualified vendors, consolidation of purchases, solicitation of competitive bids, win-win negotiation, and vendor relationships. (RELEVANT INFORMATION) A flexible training schedule is available as posted on the purchasing web site. Offerings are designed to be compatible with various sites, delivery systems, languages, and cultural characteristics. (CONSIDERS NEEDS)*

It is worth noting again that training is all too often the first step in a change project. People are ordered into a training session, sometimes with little awareness of why they are there. A far more cost-effective and instructionally-effective approach is to *prepare people for training*. Make them *aware* of what the training is about and how it may relate to their needs and concerns, give them a chance to *dialogue* regarding the content of the training, and offer them evidence or a *demonstration* of the worth of that content—all before they are thrown into training.

Even if you find yourself in an organizational situation in which training is scheduled as the first step in adopting a change, try to find ways to communicate with the trainees/adopters ahead of time or, if that isn't possible, begin the training session with an awareness activity and an elicitation of their concerns and questions. Interactive group activities are particularly useful for the latter.

For Stage 5 Adoption

With training behind them, adopters enter into the first, fumbling phase of on-the-job use. They think things like, "I could do it in training. Why isn't it working now?" And "Why didn't they teach us what we really need to know?" They need two kinds of support— *technical assistance* to get the kinks out and to help them integrate the change into their work and *rewards* for accepting yet another change and performing as desired.

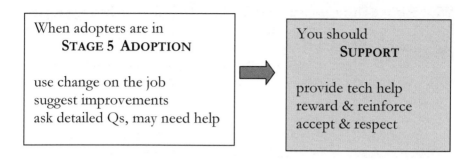

| When adopters are in **STAGE 5 ADOPTION** use change on the job suggest improvements ask detailed Qs, may need help | You should **SUPPORT** provide tech help reward & reinforce accept & respect |

How might the change agent offer the two kinds of SUPPORT to Trektel's purchasing people?

Technical assistance is provided by purchasing people from the pilot site. They are assigned as coaches. When a buyer with little negotiation experience goes into a session with a vendor, an experienced coach is a member of the team. (TECHNICAL HELP)

Rewards are provided through articles naming names in the corporate newsletter and human-interest stories in local newspapers. Given that the new purchasing procedures are a hot item in the business world, once savings begin to be realized, national business publications are contacted for possible articles. (REWARDS & RESPECT)

Technical assistance can be made available in a variety of forms, e.g., technical experts, field coaches, even the frustrating Help functions of software and automated systems. However, common problems lie either in the inadequate allocation of resources to provide technical support or the failure to identify or design an operational mechanism to supply the support.

Regarding the latter, I am reminded of a development project on which I consulted a few years ago for an online institution.

What Support?

The organization was incredibly well-funded, touted by the national news media as the ultimate online institution, and projecting many thousands of students. However, things didn't work out and before they really got going, they closed down.

I'm sure there were other reasons, but, from my viewpoint, one problem they never seemed to confront realistically was how they were going to supply the online, live support they were promising for thousands of learners. It was true that, as they said, advanced graduate students in the content fields might be able to supply the support, but how many hundreds of them were going to be needed and how were they going to be available on an as-needed basis? I never heard these questions addressed. I guess they were being saved for later.

The organization may have been lucky that "later" never came.

Rewards and reinforcement, the other kind of support, has one of the same problems, e.g., inadequate resources. If there is no time and no money, it probably won't happen. However, there is also another problem. That has to do with the nature of the rewards. Money and recognition are the two common rewards, but it may be that these are not always the best rewards, as you can see in Ken Kovach's report on differences between employees' and supervisors' rankings of rewards.

What Employees Want	What Supervisors Think Employees Want
1. Interesting work	1. Good wages
2. Full appreciation of work done	2. Job security
3. Feeling of being "in" on things	3. Promotion and growth
4. Job security	4. Good working conditions
5. Good wages	5. Interesting work
6. Promotion and growth	6. Personal loyalty to employees
7. Good working conditions	7. Tactful disciplining
8. Personal loyalty to employees	8. Full appreciation of work done
9. Tactful disciplining	9. Help with personal problems
10. Help with personal problems	10. Feeling of being "in" on things

Some of the largest discrepancies are worth noting. While employees ranked "interesting work" as higher than everything else, their supervisors ranked it only number 5. While employees ranked a "full appreciation of work done" as second, their supervisors ranked it number 8. While employees ranked a "feeling of being 'in' on things" as third, their supervisors ranked it last at number 10. All three items suggest that these employees valued their work and their jobs and wanted to be treated accordingly, but apparently their supervisors did not credit or respect them for having such values.

While this data should be taken as a warning that adopters may view rewards differently from others (e.g., managers, change agents), data gathered at other places and other times (e.g., during a downsizing or recession) might reveal a different ordering. Also perhaps items not on the list would be even more valued than these. So when you're planning rewards, it's a good idea to find out what kind of rewards your adopters value.

Some Examples of Rewards   Here are a few simple, inexpensive suggestions from Chocolate Model users.

> Jennifer O'Hartigan *In our company culture, if you are impressed with a coworker, you send an email directly to their manager and cc the coworker. This is the greatest compliment that you can receive…What an easy reward for me to incorporate into my project.*

> Randy Kirk *Money is great, but you always want more. I totally agree with the simple Kudos…I often bring cookies to Committee meetings…it's just a simple "Thanks for giving me some of your busy day to be here."…Friendly competition…where you can see other department's work according to their measurements. I nick-name these departments…"Brag Departments" It's not putting others in a bad light…it's allowing departments that are struggling to see and talk with peers and get ideas. The "Brag Departments" become mentors.*

> Tiffini Sorcic   *If your office observes a business or business casual environment, an absolutely free incentive is to allow the employees to wear jeans (and possibly tennis shoes) on a particular day/week…Of course, this only works in workplaces that can allow jeans.*

Josephine Poelma *I haven't been able to figure it out, but there is something about being able to show up for work in a pair of jeans that really gets folks excited...another incentive I've seen is letting folks work from home for a day. This is especially valued by employees who live far away.*

Ginette Lupton *...we do casual days too. Only in our case it is used as a fund-raiser (pay $2 and wear your civies). It still has a great effect on morale.*

Kelly Curry *One of the incentives I read about [in Get Weird] was about a company that would send pizza or some sort of take-out to the families of staff that had to work late. It really doesn't cost much and it sends a great message of appreciation.*

Rosabeth Moss Kanter offers reward principles which include—deliver rewards in a public way, tailor rewards to the individual, give rewards close to the time of the achievement and, most interesting of all, recognize those who recognize others. In *1001 Ways to Reward Employees*, Bob Nelson shares "1001" examples of both informal and formal rewards. He also offers an interesting formula,

For every four informal rewards (e.g., a special thank-you), there should be a more official acknowledgement (e.g., a letter of recognition), and for every four of those, there should be a still more official reward (e.g., a plaque or public praise at a company meeting), leading ultimately to more traditional rewards such as raises, bonuses, promotions, and special assignments.

Some change agents and managers cut corners on technical support and omit rewards entirely. As a result, new programs are less than effective and end up costing time and money. And workers feel unappreciated and are less cooperative when the next change comes around.

Two More Change Aids The first Change Aid summarizes strategies that match each adopter stage. The second Change Aid suggests tactics for each strategy.

Adoption Stages & Change Agent Strategies

IF adopters are in this stage   **THEN** you should

1. Awareness Advertise

are passive about the change
have little/no info. about the change
have little/no opinion about the change

get their attention
be brief and positive
appeal to their perceived needs

2. Curiosity Dialogue

are more active regarding the change
have personal concerns & opinions
ask Qs about the impact on them

elicit/listen to their concerns
respond to their concerns/Qs
provide relevant information

3. Mental Tryout Demonstrate

imagine how the change fits with their jobs
have job-focused concerns
ask Qs about task and job impact

show the change in action
provide examples of success
connect with satisfied peers

4. Hands-on Tryout Train

are ready to learn how to use change
have opinions about the change & use
ask Qs re organization & other impact

provide S/K training
accept/consider their opinions
provide relevant information

5. Adoption Support

use the change on the job
make suggestions for improvements
ask detailed questions & may need help

provide trouble shooting help
reward & reinforce
accept & respect

The preceding IF-THEN chart indicates some ways the effective change facilitator should behave. Here are some caveats, some things the change facilitator should *not* do.

Don't Skip Stages! Although adopters may not go through all of the stages and although some stages may be hard to see (e.g., mental tryout), it is best to plan for all of the stages. A common mistake is to plunge adopters into training before they are ready. This can make even the best training less than effective.

Don't Change the Order of the Stages! The linear model proposed is a simple one to learn and a good one to follow—so long as you understand that, as adopters get more information, they often cycle among stages. Plan for the five stages and monitor what's going on with the adopters as best you can, adjusting if necessary but still maintaining your overall direction.

Don't Rush Through the Stages! You may be under the gun to hurry, to bring about change on an unrealistic schedule. Top-level managers often have their own agendas. For example, the dictator, Indonesian President Sukarno, "declared" literacy so he and his country could look good and get business and assistance from the world community. He succeeded at *his* goals, but his statistics didn't mean that any more people could read and write.

Tactics to Match Strategies

For Stage 1   Advertising

announcement by high-level manager
newsletter article by credible source
contest to name the change
web page

bulletin board display
poster campaign
e-mail or Twitter teaser
YouTube video

For Stage 2   Dialogue

20 Questions flyer—answers to most-asked questions
pamphlet relating change features to positive adopter outcomes
overview presentation by credible, informed, articulate person
informal discussions with adopters held in high esteem
series on major features of the change
Q-A sessions added to regular departmental meeting agendas

For Stage 3   Demonstration

visits to successful sites
informal meetings with peer users
formal presentations by adopters/experts

adopter teleconferences
videotaped testimonials
print success stories

For Stage 4   Training

workshop
reprints of relevant articles
series of how-to flyers

how-to video
online tutorial
job aids

For Stage 5   Support

Technical

assigned on-site expert
expert available by e-mail
web-based help desk
adopter network list
troubleshooting job aid

Rewards

newsletter recognition
boss acknowledges at meeting
bonus
parking space
desired special assignment

WORKSHEET 10   Make an action plan for your project. As you can see on the following page, the plan should have seven columns and six rows. Because you will be revising or adding to your plan as you go through the book, you might want to use Excel or write in pencil on a large sheet of paper. (For examples of Action Plans, see Appendix E.)

STAGE & STRATEGY   The first column lists the five stages and the related strategies.

MESSAGE (the content)   The second column specifies exactly what you're trying to get over to your adopters at each stage. (Ex: In Kotter's glove example, at the initial Awareness stage, the CEO wanted to send his division presidents a message something like—"You're paying a lot more than you have to for your purchases." or "You're wasting your money.") For each stage, make a simple statement of what you want the adopters to hear or understand. If you can't say it in a few words, you probably aren't yet clear about what you really want to communicate. Especially in the Awareness stage, beware of trying to send too many messages.

ACTIONS (the medium)   Once you've specified the message, what action will you take to deliver it? VIP announcement? meeting? poster? e-mail? web page? Be specific but creative (like Kotter's CEO).

PEOPLE   Now that you have the message clarified and you know what actions you will take to communicate it to the adopters, whose help do you need? Do you need someone for design/development (e.g., a graphics person)? for delivery (e.g., a department head or director)?

DATES   Be as specific and realistic as you can. If the project is entirely in the future and exact dates are unknown, just say Week 1, 2, etc. to show how much time each stage will take.

RESOURCES   Again, be as specific and realistic as you can about all of the resources needed. Consider time, effort, money, etc.

LEADERSHIP   Leave blank for now.

STAGE & STRATEGY	MESSAGE	ACTIONS	PEOPLE	DATE	RESOURCES	LEADERSHIP
IF Awareness THEN Advertise						
IF Curiosity THEN Dialogue						
IF Mental Tryout THEN Demonstrate						
IF Hands-on Tryout THEN Train						
IF adoption THEN Support						

FOR FUN

Here's an example that illustrates one man's difficulty with a new bit of technology and the change agent who tries to help him. Go to

YouTube: Medieval helpdesk with English subtitles

If You Want to Read More

This is a good time to read *Kotter & Cohen's The Heart of Change*. It is organized around Kotter's 8-step leadership model (which is different from but compatible with the Chocolate Model), is very readable, and has many good stories that suggest ideas for all adopter stages. And, who knows? You might have as big a pay-off as the one Nancy Torkewitz describes here.

> *I want to share a real world, organizational example of the Kotter & Cohen quote, "People change what they do less because they are given analysis that shifts their thinking than because they are shown a truth that influences their feelings."*
>
> *About two weeks ago, Dan, the Global Lead for the Really Big Organizational Transformation project I'm involved with, asked for some help He was going to give a presentation about Really Big Project to the leaders of Syngenta's various businesses, regions, and functions all around the world. They were all going to be attending a three day conference. Also in attendance were their direct reports. In total, about 95 top dogs from all around the world. They are busy, smart, analytical, powerful people.*
>
> *This project has been in the design stage for about a year so these leaders already knew about it. Dan had 20 minutes on the agenda to update them on the status of Really Big Project. He also knew 60 minutes had been blocked out for each of the regional groups to meet to discuss next steps for their region/business units.*

Dan wanted his presentation to inspire and motivate them as they head into the actual implementation phase, which will begin in the next two months. He knew the leaders themselves will have to act differently for this business transformation to be successful. Implementation will take a lot of energy and focus.

Luckily for me, when Dan called, I had just finished reading the introduction of Heart of Change. I talked to him about the relative advantages of see-feel-change vs. analyze-think-change that was central to the book (he had not read it but said he'd pick up a copy).

I persuaded him to scrap most of the charts and graphs and other data in his presentation. We then talked about ways to get the leaders to see the change. What we decided to do was use pictures that related to particular human emotions they might be feeling as they were about to step into the scary, difficult implementation phase.

What happened?

Dan's presentation was the most talked-about in the entire three day conference. The leaders opened up in their break out groups and acknowledged the human emotions they were feeling and thus how the people in their regions might feel when they headed into this change.

For example, after Dan gave some information about time lines, he used a really funny picture of a baby monkey who looks like he's thinking "Are you KIDDING ME?" It generated laughs and broke the tension.

One picture in particular that people referred to over and over again was a photo of a surfer riding in front of this humongous wave. They talked about what it must have felt like just before he paddled out and started to ride the wave. The wave could crash on the surfer at any moment, yet you had the sense that the guy was going to make it. They all wanted to be that surfer who surely was fully aware of the huge wave, yet was confident that he could do it.

That metaphor/visualization will stick with them long beyond the conference. It was a great example of this statement in Heart of Change:

"Successful see-feel-change tactics tend to be clever, not clumsy, and never cynically manipulative. They often have an afterglow, where the story of the event is told over and over again or where there is a remaining visible sign of the event that influences additional people over time."

Dan was really happy about how the whole thing went and I had a "Thank you, John Kotter, for making us look good!" moment.

Whether or not you decide to read *The Heart of Change*, this anecdote makes a point emphasized by many change experts. Kotter and Cohen say you need to help people not to analyze-*think*-change, but to see-*feel*-change. The Heath brothers say you need to activate, not just people's Rider (the rational side), but their Elephant (the emotional side). And long before these authors were offering advice on how to have an impact, Henry James wrote a note to himself in the margin of one of his manuscripts—"Dramatize, dramatize!"

Note: If you have left-brain adopters (e.g., engineers), you may need to present the facts, the data, the rationale regarding your change early on, but for most adopters (even engineers), you will get their attention best with visual or verbal images that tap into their feelings.

8. More Tactics—New & Old

In the last chapter, you got high-level *strategies* for each adoption stage and, for each strategy, you also got some related *tactics*. For example, when adopters are in Stage 1 Awareness, the suggested strategy is Advertise. Some tactics suggested were an announcement by a high-level manager, a newsletter article by a credible source, a bulletin board display, a poster campaign, a contest to name the change, an e-mail or Twitter teaser, a web page and a YouTube video. You may have noticed that these suggestions range from traditional presentation-and-print to online tactics that have been possible only in the last few years. This chapter elaborates on a group of these newer tactics which are inevitable, as well as on one old tactic which has stood the test of time.

The New—Online Media

E-Mail

Today, E-mail is probably the simplest and the most used of the online media. But given the flood of daily e-mails, it's hard for any one of them to get much attention. However, people do notice the e-mail that appeals to their interests, needs and—most of all—emotions. In *The Dragonfly Effect*, Jennifer Aaker and Andy Smith offer a directive on how to write such a message.

How to Write an Email That Inspires
Action and Spurs Change

Make it personal. *Include accessible and specific details about the person or cause you're trying to help. Give someone a reason to care.*

Make it informative. *Use e-mail as an opportunity to educate your audience.*

Make it direct. *Specifically ask the recipients for help, tell them what you want them to do, and give them all the tools they need to do it easily.*

Consider this example of what an e-mail can do to bring about change.

Sameer Bhatia was thirty-one, running a Silicon Valley gaming company, and newly married when he was diagnosed with an extremely aggressive form of leukemia—acute myelogenous leukemia or AML. After a few months of chemotherapy and medication, he was told that his only chance for survival was a bone marrow transplant.

Such transplants require a tissue match which is most likely to be found in a close relative or, failing that, in a donor of the same ethnicity. In Sameer's case, no relatives matched so he turned to the National Marrow Donor Program, a database with 8,000,000 potential donors registered. Caucasians have a 1 in 15 chance of finding a match in the databank. However, because such a small percentage of South Asians were registered. Sameer's chance of finding a match was 1 in 20,000. (Although India itself has 1.2 billion people, they have no comprehensive bone marrow registry.) No match for Sameer was found and he had only a few months left.

If you look at this situation as a change project, you can see that the targeted people were thousands of South Asians and the change they needed to adopt was registration in the national donor database. And the adoption needed to occur quickly. This is when a "change agent" stepped in. Sameer's friend, Robert Chatwani, decided to solicit registrations by sending an e-mail to their close Asian friends.

"Dear Friends, Please take a moment to read this e-mail. My friend, Sameer Bhatia, has been diagnosed with Acute Myelogenous Leukemia (AML), which is cancer of the blood. He is in urgent need of a bone marrow transplant."

Robert's e-mail went on to tell about Sameer's new marriage, his diagnosis, his accomplishments, his charitable activities (PERSONAL) including a microfinance fund that his readers would recognize had helped, among other, many Asians. (MORE REASONS TO CARE) Then, it described the bone marrow availability situation (INFORMATIVE) and repeated what Sameer needed.

"He is undergoing chemotherapy at present but needs a bone marrow transplant to sustain [his life] beyond the next few months."

Last, Robert told the recipients exactly what they could do to help (DIRECTION TO ACT):

*1. **Please get registered.** He included instructions on how to do this and a link to local locations.*

*2. **Spread the word.** He asked recipients to share the e-mail with 10 others and to ask them to do the same. He told about local bone-marrow drives and asked that they organize one in their companies or communities. He reminded them that the drives needed to take place in the next 2-3 weeks.*

*3. **Learn more.** He provided the link to a site with details on how to organize a drive, information about AML, and a success story about an Indian woman who had fought AML.*

He ended by thanking the recipients for their help in the fight against leukemia, and he signed his first name. (STILL MAKING IT PERSONAL)

Dud Robert make it "personal, informative, and direct"? Indeed he did. Can you do the same? (Needless to say, asking people to buy into a new software system is a long way from asking someone to help one of their own whose life is in jeopardy.) Here's a version of the Aaker & Smith directive adapted a bit for organizational change projects.

How to Write an Email to Inspire Change

Make it personal. Include a few attention-getting details about the change that are of interest to the adopters. Give adopters a reason to care, to *feel*.

Make it informative. Briefly, clarify what the change is. (But not too much information.)

Make it realistic. Don't sugarcoat or set up expectations that can't be delivered on later.

Make it directive. Tell adopters specifically what will happen next and, if you want them to do something (e.g., come to a meeting, post questions on a blog), tell them, and be sure they have the tools to do it.

WORKSHEET 11 **Write an e-mail to introduce your change.** Whether or not you intend to use such an e-mail in your project, draft a *brief* message to introduce the change (Awareness). You may find this easier if you aim it at your opinion leader and/or key innovator. Make it *personal* (What's in it for them? How does it relate to them? What emotion do you want them to feel?), *informative* (But not too much information at this first stage), *realistic* (Don't promise more than you can deliver.), and *directive* (What do you really want them to do after they read your message?). This activity can help you think more clearly about any message or activity you may later create to introduce the change.

Social Networks

Given the size of his targeted group and the criticality of the change he wanted, Robert didn't stop with a few e-mails. He and others moved on to more complex activities facilitated through more sophisticated online media, including social networks.

Along with other friends, Robert organized an Internet campaign that, in two days, reached 35,000 South Asians via e-mail. These messages turned into a Help Sameer campaign that used Facebook, Google Apps, and YouTube to develop bone marrow drives across the nation. Soon almost 25,000 South Asians had registered with the database. A donor was found for Sameer.

Facebook is one example of a mediated social network. Let's compare it to the earlier definition of a social system given by Rogers.

> *A social system is a set of interrelated units that are engaged in joint problem solving to accomplish a common goal. A system has structure, defined as the patterned arrangements of the units in a system, which gives stability and regularity to individual behavior in a system. The social and communication structure of a system facilitates or impedes the diffusion of innovations in the system.*

As was evident with Sameer's situation, Facebook can be used "in joint problem solving." It has "units" which are "interrelated" electronically in a "patterned arrangement," giving "stability and regularity to individual behavior." It can be used to "facilitate or impede the diffusion of an innovation." (For example, within minutes of availability, Facebook users with an interest knew the Apple iPad's strengths and weaknesses.)

So Facebook does qualify as a Rogerian social system, but does this mean that we can apply what we know about face-to-face social systems to virtual social networks? For example, do key adopters—opinion leaders, innovators, traditionalists—exist in a group of Facebook "friends"? Can Gladwell's mavens, connectors, and salesmen be identified among such distant adopters? Although to my knowledge, no one has yet studied this kind of question, we might speculate by returning to Robert's change project which involved a virtual community.

Robert's adopters numbered in the thousands, but he didn't begin by sending an e-mail to all of them. He began by targeting a sub-group—close friends, people most likely to buy into helping Sameer. In a Chocolate Model framework, we might view the members of this sub-group as the Innovators and Early Adopters from the larger group. Then, as these close friends sent e-mails to dozens of their friends and organized donor drives, some of them probably began to function as opinion leaders and as Gladwell's mavens, connectors and salesmen. (Of course, some may also have begun to function as traditionalists who objected to the change.)

Transferring this to a change project in which a sizeable group of adopters exists in a virtual organization, the change agent might ask the following questions:

Q Is there a sub-set of the larger adopter group (a) which might be responsive to the change, (b) which is either respected or viewed neutrally by the larger group, and (c) which has a positive relationship with the change agent or sponsor?

Q Can this sub-set of adopters be enlisted to contact, inform, and persuade others? Can the entire membership of the larger group be reached in this cascading way?

Another important aspect of a change project is feedback.

Q How can the change agent get feedback about the concerns, questions, attitudes, actions, etc. of members of the sub-group and of the larger group of adopters?

Although these questions are not that different from those asked in a face-to-face change situation, since the use of online social networking in organizational change projects is just beginning, the answers and examples are not so readily available. Nevertheless, with an awareness that a group's receptivity may vary according to demographics, social networking and other online media are almost certainly tactics worth exploring, especially if you are trying to bring about change in virtual groups such as those found in nation-wide or global organizations.

If You Want to Read More

While I know of no currently available books that directly relate online social networks to facilitating *organizational* change, a number of books relate them to facilitating *social* change. One of these is Jennifer Aaker and Andy Smith's *The Dragonfly Effect: Quick, Effective, and Powerful Ways to Use Social Media to Drive Social Change* which offers a number of practical suggestions that are adaptable to organizational change efforts—e.g., how to create a Facebook page or YouTube video to elicit the desired action on the part of the recipients.

The Old—Storytelling

While you're figuring how to use the latest online media, don't forget one of the oldest communication tools of all time—a story.

Whether the storytellers are Harvard Business School faculty with case studies or kindergarten teachers with Dr. Seuss, the best teachers, parents, presenters, and change agents use stories as a way to connect with their audiences.

> *Tell me the facts and I'll learn. Tell me the truth and I'll believe. But tell me a story and it will live in my heart forever.*

John Kotter knows this and *The Heart of Change* is filled with good stories. Malcolm Gladwell knows this and all of his best-sellers include stories. Tom Friedman knows this; he can even pack a story into a short title. *The World Is Flat* may seem obvious now, but when it came out in 2005, the use of an ancient idea to bring up the picture of a global world that has been flattened and made accessible to all because of the technological revolution was, in itself, an attention-getting story. Jennifer Aaker, co-author of *The Dragonfly Effect*, knows this and teaches a course at Stanford's School of Business on "How to Tell a Story."

When Should You Tell a Story? While a good story could be used at any stage of adoption, it seems especially suitable for Stage 1 Awareness. In this first stage, you need to Advertise—to get the adopters' attention, to be brief and positive, and to appeal to their needs. What better way than to tell a quick story?

A great example of story-telling-to-advertise is Steve Jobs' introduction of the 1984 Mac.

A televised ad was designed to be shown during the Superbowl and to be shown publicly only this once. The ad used the widespread recognition of George Orwell's novel—*Nineteen Eighty Four*—and set up IBM as Big Brother, the heartless dictator who, through an onscreen presence, commanded the robot-like masses. But then, a woman athlete appeared, running toward the screen. With a hammer in her hand and an Apple logo on her shirt, she demolished the onscreen dictator and brought freedom to the world. The world (or at least the vast Superbowl audience) became aware that the Mac was on its way!

In one YouTube version, you can see Jobs' preview of the ad at Apple's annual meeting for all employees. You can hear how the employees respond and you can imagine how the subsequent Superbowl audience will respond. Even if you've seen it before, watch it again, imagine yourself back in the 1984 audience that had long viewed IBM as the absolute ruler in the computer industry, and think about how this video's impact illustrates the effectiveness of a good story to get attention and introduce a change.

YouTube — 1983 Apple keynote

What Kind of Story Should You Tell?   In *The Leader's Guide to Storytelling: Mastering the Art and Discipline of Business Narrative,* Stephen Denning says that the kind of story you tell depends on the purpose you have in telling it. He describes eight kinds, each for a different purpose. (See End Note)

When your purpose is to "ignite action and implement new ideas," as it is in Advertising, Denning recommends the "springboard" form of story which is always...

- related to the change
- true
- simply told
- positive

It Relates to the Change.   Obviously, the story you tell should somehow connect with the change you want them to adopt. But, it's up to you to make it fit as much as possible.

There are many (honest) ways to tell the same story. However, the details you select and the ordering of events can emphasize or dilute the relevance of the story to your change. Select details to make the point you want to make. Arrange and order them to dramatize their relevance to your change.

It's True.   Look for a true story. In her course syllabus on storytelling in business settings, Aaker provides a hint about where to find a true story.

> *This question becomes important for leaders of companies, who often only need to act as an editor - shaping the stories told by employees and customers...*

Look for stories that already exist in your organization and in other organizations where your change or similar changes have been implemented.

Suggestion! If you can't find a true story in your own organization, borrow one that makes your point, the way I've been doing throughout this book.

It's Simply Told.   Use a simple and direct style, get rid of unnecessary details, and avoid qualifiers which distract and weaken your message.

In college, were you ever assigned a scholarly article that you found hard to get through? One reason for this is that academics have a professional responsibility not only to tell the whole truth about their topics, but to include all possible qualifiers. Unfortunately this often leaves their prose impenetrable for the uninitiated. While honesty really is the best policy, it's neither necessary nor desirable to tell everything, especially at the early stages of adoption. You might take a hint from Peter Drucker who, when criticized for an exaggeration, said, "I use anecdotes to make a point, not to write history."

It's Positive. With the springboard story, Denning says you must have a positive tone. He supports his position with brain research.

> *...if I tell the audience a story with an unhappy ending...what seems to be happening is that this ancient part of the brain, the limbic system, kicks in and the message is "Trouble! Something bad is happening! Do something! Fight! Flee!"...But by contrast, if I tell a story with a happy ending, what seems to be happening is that the limbic system kicks in with something called an "endogenous opiate reward" for the human brain, the cortex. It pumps a substance called dopamine into the cortex...This leads to a warm and floaty feeling, the kind of mild euphoria that you have after a wonderful movie. And this is the perfect frame of mind to be thinking about a new future..."*

Christa Ledbetter designed a simple, energizing awareness activity built on a positive story, one told in pictures.

> *The organization Christa worked in was a not-for-profit agency dealing with developmental disabilities. The agency included 30 therapists supervised by a director who was long-established, highly competent, and extremely well-liked. However, because of rapid growth, the agency was being reorganized and the director was going to move on. A new director was chosen to take her place. The 30 therapists (the adopters) were almost certain to view such a change as a negative event. The task for Christa was to come up with a way to help them see the change in a positive light.*

Her approach (see the next page) is reminiscent of that taken by Steve Jobs' except Christa's presentation of a positive story was via a poster which used clip art and cost only pennies. The poster (originally in color) offered a positive vision of the change-over (passing the torch from one winning-looking woman to another) and invited the adopters to a celebration with the old and new directors. An additional strength of Christa's awareness activity is that, after individuals saw the poster, they were invited to come together at a celebration. And when they got there, they would all have a positive story in their heads.

In Sum When you're trying to attract adopters to your change, a story can be a big help. This is true whether you use *real objects* like the CEO's gloves, a *video* like Steve Jobs' Superbowl ad, *pictures* like those on Christa's poster, or just plain *words* like Martin Luther King's "I Have a Dream" speech.

The Passing of the Torch!!!

You're invited to the Passing of the Torch party!
Come celebrate with Tracy and Michelle as the exciting change
takes place.
Learn how this change will ensure company growth, service to
children and job security.
July 7
5:30 PM
Conference Room
You bring the excitement, we'll bring the refreshments.

How Should You Tell a Story? Once you've identified a true story that shows your change in a positive light, how do you tell it?

Set a conversational tone. Whether the message is delivered as a live presentation, a video, or in some other medium, it should sound and feel as if you are holding a conversation with the adopter. Of course, appearing spontaneous doesn't mean that you can wing it. Denning says "the preparation for a storytelling performance is laborious and repetitive....The perfection comes from practice, while the spontaneity comes from reliving the story mentally for each retelling."

The more important the change, the more time and effort you may need to spend. Think of Sameer's friend Robert who worked for hours to get that first brief message just right. Think of Steve Jobs and imagine how much of his and others' efforts went into that Superbowl presentation. Edit and rewrite, test your message on others, revise until it says exactly what you want it to say in exactly the way you want it to be said. If you are the one delivering the message, rehearse until it is second nature. If your boss or CEO is delivering the message, do the best you can to help and to optimize the message and the venue.

Use media effectively. All media can be used well or poorly. Back in the day of overhead transparencies (which involved a pull-off sheet of aluminum foil), IBM trainers used 100's of transparencies in a single training session which resulted in their trainees referring to these sessions as "Death by foil!" Today's PowerPoint slides can be just as deadly. Denning wisely recommends they be used to *convey images* or as minimalist *prompts* to keep the presenter on track. Do not fill screen after screen with words, words, words. It's boring!

Emphasize adopter benefits. You've heard this before, but it's important enough to repeat. Denning says,

> *One key area to focus on is the audience's interests: What's in it for them? How do they stand to gain or lose?...tell a story that draws attention to benefits ...and is frank about risk to the audience. Another area is the role that the audience is going to play in the change process and how it will affect them.*

If You Want to Read More Although effective leaders, presenters, and others have always used stories to make their organizational points, books on the topic have been few until the last decade or so. Now there are many relevant books on storytelling. Among them are Denning's *The Leader's Guide to Storytelling*, Annette Simmons' *The Story Factor*, and Lori Silverman's edited collection, *Wake Me Up When the Data Is Over* (neat title!).

WORKSHEET 12 Write a brief story that presents your change in a positive way. As Denning says, if you can't think of one, "Think harder."

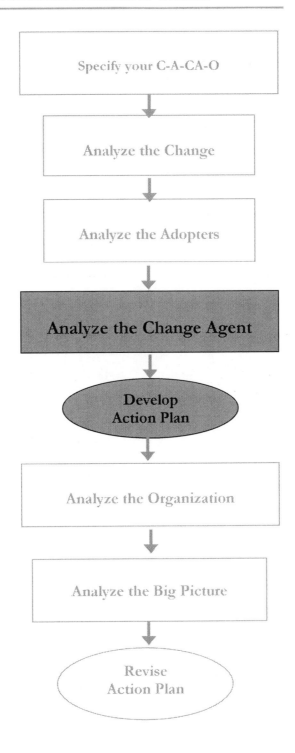

9. The CHANGE AGENT Team

Up to now, the focus has been on the needs, concerns, and problems of the adopters and their relationship to the change. But what about the change agent? Rogers begins his chapter on change agents with this quote,

> *One of the greatest pains to human nature is the pain of a new idea....Naturally, therefore, common men hate a new idea, and are disposed more or less to ill-treat the original man who brings it.*

Walter Bagehot, 1893

Times haven't changed since 1893. People rarely welcome with open arms the person who informs them that they must change. In fact, they often take a quite different position—*Kill the messenger!*

Part of a change agent's success lies in counteracting and overcoming this view. This requires not only managing people and resources, but also a wide variety of *skills and knowledge*, as well as certain *personal attributes*. The job involves juggling a lot of things!

Skills & Knowledge Needed

Change agents need a wide range of expertise. This includes the skills and knowledge associated with the adopter group, data-gathering, communication, technical aspects of the change, training, leadership, the organization and change agentry.

Adopter Expertise

As you've learned in previous chapters, it's all-important that you understand the adopters and their relationship to the change. This not only takes skill, but it is time-consuming.

Before you protest that you can't afford all that time, consider what change consultant Daryl Conner says, "Pay now or pay later." Spend time at the front end of a change project or spend time later dealing with problems you didn't need to have.

Data-Gathering Skills

You can't really understand the adopters and their relationship to the change without getting first-hand data. Data-gathering methods include informal observations, interviews and questionnaires. Each involves its own set of skills. Data-gathering also involves issues which can be critical to the relationship between the change agent and others. Here are some of those:

- **Vulnerability** Asking people to tell you what they really think about a mandated change places them in a vulnerable position. Are you prepared to protect them?

- **Trust** Why should adopters tell you the truth? Why should they trust you? *Can* they trust you? with their words? with their well-being?

- **Time Required** Gathering data takes time—yours and theirs. Short cuts (e.g., e-mail questionnaires) are a possibility but may produce less valid data.

- **Interpretations of the Data** This is always tricky. Avoid using data like a drunk uses a lamppost—for support rather than for illumination.

- **Impact of the Data** Is the data really going to affect the change? or the way the change is implemented?

- **Value** Is there a payoff for the adopters? for the organization?

Communication Skills

This class of skills is so broad and so basic to the adoption process that it is tempting to say that it is the most important skill set needed. Jack Welch said that, even after the changes he instigated at GE were well underway, one of his biggest surprises was how much and how often he had to communicate with the people in the organization.

Of all the communication skills needed, the most important one is *listening*. Sivasailam "Thiagi" Thiagarajan says, "You don't bring about change by talking. You bring it about by listening." Don't think about what you're going to say next, focus on what the other person is saying. In addition to skill at listening, the change agent needs skill at *sending*—for example, in face-to-face presentations and meetings, in print and electronic communiqués, in video productions. Two factors to consider in all of these are the *sender* of the message and the *medium* used for the communication.

The Sender Matters!   In interpersonal exchanges, people communicate most easily with others who are like them in such characteristics as beliefs, occupations, education, etc. Rogers says that "Talking with others who are markedly different requires more effort to make communication effective." As has already been pointed out, change agents are often different from their targeted adopters. In such a case, effective *listening* is especially valuable for bridging the gap. Another solution is to enlist an opinion leader who is enough like the other adopters to communicate easily with them.

The Medium Matters! (and it matters differently at different times) Whether the message is sent via mass media or via interpersonal exchanges can make a difference. *Mass media* (e.g., publications, videos, electronic media) is best used to *get attention* and *provide information* about the change. Hence, it is well-suited for the early stages of adoption—Awareness and Curiosity. *Interpersonal exchanges* (e.g., adopter discussions with opinion leaders and peer users) are best used to *persuade* people to accept the change. Hence, they are best used in the later stages of adoption, especially in the third stage of Mental Tryout.

Example Of Success   No contemporary group has taken better advantage of these principles than the organizers of the 2008 Obama presidential campaign as summarized by Tim Dickinson in a *Rolling Stone* article. (Ignore the politics, just consider the strategies.)

> *Over the past year, the Obama campaign has quietly worked to integrate the online technologies…with the kind of neighbor-to-neighbor movement-building that Obama learned as a young organizer on the streets of Chicago…They've married the incredibly powerful online community they built with real on-the-ground field operations.*

They used the internet upfront for *mass communication* but later made *interpersonal contact* with "old-fashioned shoe-leather, door-knocking."

Rumors count!   Be aware that the first rumor a potential adopter hears marks the beginning of the adoption process. Jeanie Daniel Duck describes the way many companies approach change—the CEO decides that a change is required and appoints a task force, the task force doesn't tell anyone what they're doing. They assume "We haven't said anything yet, so we're not really communicating." Duck says,

> *Everything that is or is not done sends a message. The original announcement that change is on its way sends a message…Even the appointment of the task force…sends an important message…When the task force chooses not to inform the rest of the organization about its work, it is saying, 'We're busy figuring out your future—we'll tell you what it is when we're ready.'*

The result is that people talk, rumors get passed around, and they're often more negative than reality would be.

Continuity counts! It's not just the quantity, quality and medium that matter; it's also the continuity—*for the receiver of the message.* What was the last thing potential adopters or sponsors heard or read about the change or the change project? That's where their heads will be when they receive the next message, but change agents often send so many messages that they're only aware of the last message *sent,* when what matters is the last message the other person *receive*d. Stop and think about "where the receiver is" before you send another message.

Technical Expertise

You—and/or a technical expert—should understand the specifics of the change and be available to the potential adopters, particularly at the beginning and the end of a change effort. At the beginning, if potential adopters are not to horribilize, they need accurate information. Later, when they are using the change on the job and have technical questions or problems, they need access to technical expertise.

Since many organizational changes today are technological, IT personnel are often the source of the expertise needed. However, such technical experts often speak a different language from front-line users. Peter Drucker said that being a knowledge worker "demands for the first time in history that people with knowledge take responsibility for making themselves understood by people who do not have the same knowledge base."

Since all too few techies know how to translate for non-techies, change agents may find themselves in the middle between the experts and the adopters and need to serve as a linker between the two. One commentator aptly said that change agents must speak many "organizational languages."

Note also that there is an inclination to assume that the more complex the change, the more technical effort will be needed. However, as it turns out, the more complex the change, the more likely that additional *political,* rather than technical, effort will be needed.

Training Expertise

For all but the simplest changes, training will probably be called for. The resources for providing adopters with the skills and knowledge needed to use the change effectively must be identified and enlisted. For some change agents, this means collaborating with the internal training department or with an external consulting group. Again, the change agent may need to serve as a linker between adopters and the training providers. Regardless of who provides it, training should be performance-oriented and based on a reliable instructional design approach. (See End Note)

Leadership Attributes

The change project may live or die on the basis of leadership. The word "attributes" is used here to encompass not only skills, but organizational position. For example, sponsors and opinion leaders can offer important leadership in a change project, but that is initially because of their position within the organization or group. Of course, they still need the skills associated with leadership. And, when appropriate, others—such as the technical expert or the change agent —may be in a position to offer leadership also. (Leadership is addressed in more detail in Chapter 10.)

Organizational Expertise

To succeed as a change agent, you need to know the culture and traditions of the organization (or, at least, the part of it in which your adopters work). You also need to know any current strategies or initiatives that may relate to your change as well as the organizational structure and how your adopters fit in. (Organizational factors are addressed in more detail in Chapter 11.)

And, of course, you should know the spheres of influence and power as they relate to your change effort and to be able to work effectively with authority figures, especially your project's sponsors and your adopters' bosses. This kind of skill and knowledge can be summed up by saying you need political savvy—the more the better.

Change Agentry Expertise

Change agentry is the content of this book. Hopefully, after reading and doing the activities, you will have the basic skills and knowledge required of a change agent. If you're fortunate, others you work with will share your perspective. When this is not the case, you may find it useful from time to time to introduce them to some of the principles of change agentry. But be careful not to "jargon" them to death.

Personal Attributes

A change agent's effectiveness not only depends on skills and knowledge, but on certain personal attributes. These include *credibility*, *empathy*, and *ethics*.

Credibility   When change agents lack credibility with the adopters, they operate from a weakened position. As noted earlier, credibility can be viewed as being of two kinds: expertise and trustworthiness.

Change agents who present themselves as knowledgeable *experts* about the change had better be what they say they are. Adopters are often all too ready to catch false or erroneous statements about the new thing or about their own adoption situation. It's far better to say "I don't know, but I'll find out" or even "I don't know, what do you think?" than to be caught in a misrepresentation or a just-plain-wrong statement. Once the adopters have cause to doubt, it's hard to rebuild their confidence. As noted, the need for accurate knowledge about the change is especially important at the beginning and the end of the adoption process.

Change agents who are significantly different from the adopters—in education, organizational status, or other relevant characteristics—are likely to be seen as not entirely *trustworthy*. This is why opinion leaders from the adopter group are so valuable. They are usually trusted not to have hidden agendas insofar as the change goes.

However, if a "different" kind of change agent is the only one available, two approaches may help. First, *listening* is always a good way to go. Real listening can help most relationships. The one between a change agent and an adopter is no different. People tend to trust others who care enough to really listen. Another approach is *mirroring*. That is, to adapt one's speech, one's manner, and even one's dress to match those of the adopter. The problem in doing this is that the change agent may be seen as a phony and then the situation will only be made worse. Only when the mirroring is *unobtrusive and coupled with authentic respect* is it likely to work.

Empathy   Empathy with adopters is positively related to a change agent's success with a change project. But what is empathy? According to the dictionary, it is "the capacity for participation in another's feelings or ideas." If you have it, you are able to "get into the other fellow's shoes," "to see where the other person is coming from."

Donald Kirkpatrick, best known for his levels of evaluation, also wrote *How To Manage Change Effectively*, which has an entire chapter on empathy. In it, he wrote

> *I have often asked fishermen, "What is the most important quality of a successful fisherman?" The most frequent answer is "patience." The correct answer is "empathy"—the ability to put one's self in the place of the fish, to know where they are and what they are most apt to bite on at that particular time.*

Although this is an engaging quote, the reality is that fishermen *and* change agents need patience as well as empathy, and both are often in short supply. As for empathy, one problem is that—to some extent—either you have it or you don't. In fact, some recent neurological evidence suggests that empathy is wired in, if not at birth, soon after. So, what can you do if you are not a person who readily sees and connects with how other people feel and think?

My own view is that, if you are not a naturally empathetic person, you will never be as good at reading and connecting with other people as the naturally empathetic person, but, if you want to, you can get better. You can learn and deliberately use effective techniques for observing and listening and for understanding "where the other person is coming from."

Let me offer an extreme case to make my point.

I knew a man—let's call him Carl—for a decade in occasional social gatherings. I realized that Carl was always somewhat apart from the group but, since he was also always behind his camera, I didn't think too much about it.

Then, one day, I got a call that his wife had died under extreme circumstances and I went to their home to offer my condolences to the family. I was surprised when he pressed me to come in and sit with him alone, and I was even more surprised when he spent the next hour and a half talking. He explained that the reason he was not showing the emotional distress people might expect in the situation was because he had Asperger Syndrome.

[Wikipedia says "The lack of demonstrated empathy is possibly the most dysfunctional aspect of Asperger syndrome. Individuals with AS experience difficulties in basic elements of social interaction, which may include …a lack of social or emotional reciprocity, and impaired nonverbal behaviors in areas such as eye contact, facial expression, posture, and gesture."]

Carl said that he had been diagnosed as an adult and, only then, had learned that he could learn a set of rules for what-to-do in social situations. He went into some detail about how he had mental lists of behaviors suitable for various situations. I realized then that his role as photographer was one way he had learned to function at social events. (Note: Not every family photographer has Asperger's.)

Although he was never going to be able to empathize—to feel what others felt, Carl goes to a great deal of trouble to learn how to recognize what others need or expect and to respond appropriately.

So—why am I making such a point of this? Because I have no doubt that those of you who are good at empathizing will do so with your adopters. In fact, you probably can't keep from empathizing with them. But I'm hoping that those of you who are not especially good at it will learn from my friend Carl that—no matter how lacking you are in empathy—if you want to, you can get better at letting others know you recognize their situation.

How? Kirkpatrick offers one technique, the "Know Factor Ballot." It's a list of more than twenty areas which a change facilitator should consider regarding the adopters in a change project. The areas include routine items such as name and nickname, marital status, children, formal education, and work experience, but also such non-routine items as religion, politics, attitudes toward the company, the boss, and the union, problems outside the plant, friends at the plant, financial situation, and ambitions and goals. Kirkpatrick wrote in 1985 and, given current laws and personnel policies, many of the items he listed would no longer be acceptable areas of direct investigation, but much of this information can be acquired without direct questioning. Also, a more appropriate list could be created. It's the idea that matters—make a list of what you should know about each person involved and find out.

Again, this must sound like a lot of work. It is! As the best change agents and consultants know, it not only takes a lot of skill to interact effectively with people, it takes a lot of time and effort. No one has ever made this point better for me than a student once did.

Joe Was Right!

For several weeks in a graduate course on organizational consulting, we had been discussing Edgar Schein's approach to consulting—process consultation. The approach emphasizes the importance of interpersonal relations among the consultant, the client and the client's system and clearly takes a lot of time and effort on the part of the consultant.

At one evening class, as we sat around the conference table, one of the students—I'll call him Joe—leaned over, put his hand on my arm, and said in a frustrated tone, "But, Diane, I don't like people."

We all knew that Joe's interests and goals were on becoming a rigorous researcher, but we also knew that he was very likeable. So, while we were shocked at his comment, we were also fascinated. He must have seen from our faces that we were waiting for an explanation.

With a sigh, he added, "They take so much energy."

All I could say was, "Joe, you're right!"

People do take energy. And it's no wonder that those who are responsible for guiding multiple change efforts tend to burn out!

Ethics   When charged with the job of facilitating a change touted to be good (and what sponsor says a proposed change is not good), the change agent might ask early on, "Good for whom?" If you are asked to implement changes which you believe are not in the best interests of your adopters or even of your organization, you have a problem. Failure to get additional information about the merits and demerits of the change is likely to make you vulnerable not only to challenges from your adopters and guilt from your conscience but, eventually, even to criticism from higher management. In the worst case scenario, those in charge may have just picked you as a scapegoat.

Assuming that the change is moral, worthy, and aligned with the organizational purpose, you still have the problem of finding and using the power necessary to get the job done. Kotter says,

> *The power one needs comes, of necessity, in many forms. It has multiple bases, including ones associated with information or knowledge, good working relationships, personal skills, intelligent agendas for action, resource networks, and good track records.*

Power—in whatever form—can be used for good ends. And that's ethical.

The Change Team

You may have noticed that teamwork was not included in the list of expertise. The reason is because I've been writing as if the change agent was just one person. However, by now, it should be clear that one person would have to be a Renaissance man or woman to have all of the skills and knowledge needed, not to mention the time and energy, to do the job. The reality is that, with all but the most trivial organizational changes, the job requires a team.

One chapter in *The Wisdom of Teams*, Katzenbach and Smith's popular book on team-building, is titled "Teams and Major Change: An Inevitable Combination." The inevitability of this combination is related to

- the broad *demands* of the change agent role and

- the *benefits* that accrue from having representatives of various perspectives involved in the planning and implementation, perhaps even in the design, of the change.

With a simple small-scale change, the team may consist of just the change agent and representatives of the adopter group. With a complex large-scale change, the team may be a corporate-wide committee. Whether small or large, formal or informal, the job of implementing, and even of designing, an organizational change is best done by an appropriately constituted, effective team.

In *The Heart of Change*, Kotter and Cohen write,

> *A powerful guiding group has two characteristics. It is made up of the right people, and it demonstrates teamwork. Bu the "right people," we mean individuals with the appropriate skills, the leadership capacity, the organizational credibility, and the connections to handle a specific kind of organizational change.*

In addition to having all of the expertise needed, effective change teams have *representatives from the relevant stakeholder groups*. And, whoever is involved, the change agent is likely to have the responsibility of facilitating their becoming an effective, functional team.

In the following example, both skills sets and stakeholders are represented in the change team. (This is a real case with the names changed.)

The Madison-Whyte Case

Madison-Whyte is an electrical distributor with 1300 employees and 34 branches. When the company president, Jeremy Whyte, received the annual report from their trade association, he was shocked. For the first time in two decades, data from comparable companies across the nation showed that Madison-Whyte's gross margin had fallen from the first quartile to the second quartile. (Gross margin = the difference between cost and selling price.) Whyte saw the drop as a warning sign. The company was headed for trouble. Whyte immediately added pricing to the other problems on the agenda for the next Executive Committee meeting.

At that meeting, an agreement was reached that pricing should have the top priority. They also agreed that, to be most effective, the design of such a system needed to take into consideration the experience of the field agents who set prices for the customer, the data-management expertise of the IT group, the perspective of the marketing and sales groups, and the leadership to get the new system accepted. One member of the executive committee, the VP of Operations, was appointed as the Champion of the pricing change effort.

The Change = *a new pricing system still to be designed.*

The Adopters = *the field agents who, in the past, have had considerable liberty in setting prices for customers.*

The Sponsor = *VP of Operations or Project Champion*

The Change Agent Team = *the Gross Margin Improvement Team composed of representatives from IT, marketing, sales, and the branches where the adopters work*

As shown in the following organizational chart, an 11-member team was created with representatives from every group that would be affected by the change.

The adopters were represented by four of their managers. The manager of the top-performing branch was appointed the formal team leader. Having the VP who was sponsoring the change as a participating member (but not the formal leader) was an unusual, added advantage.

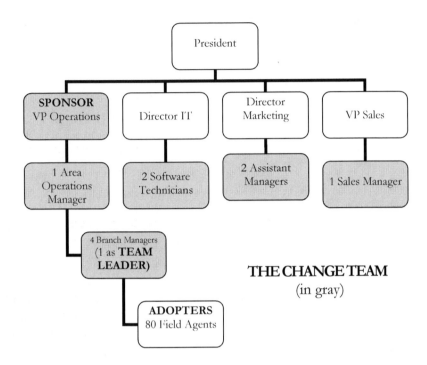

THE CHANGE TEAM
(in gray)

The Gross Margin Improvement Team (the change team) met every few weeks. In keeping with the company's accountability-based process, some 30 tasks were identified and assigned with timelines to team members who then took the lead on specific tasks. Tasks included such items as (1) create a price-override report indicating price-changes made by field agents throughout the company, (2) identify prices which should not be changed, (3) initiate an IT lockdown on those prices.

Project management software and a live networked web site kept all members informed in real time about progress. Using the latest web site data, the VP/Team Champion made a monthly status report to the Executive Committee. By the end of four months, the team had not only identified pricing loopholes but it had gathered and processed enough data to recommend that a corporate-level job be created, that of Pricing Manager. The branch manager who had been Team Leader was selected by the Executive Committee to fill that role. His work over the next year culminated in recommendations to the Executive Committee related to the establishment of corporate-wide pricing standards and the dissemination of pricing criteria to the branches and to IT.

The Madison-Whyte case is a good example of effective sponsorship, involvement, leadership, and communication.

- **Sponsorship**   Effective sponsorship was assured through the selection of a top-level "champion" with the authority to select, empower, and support the project team. His attendance at all meetings (unusual for sponsors) was a constant reminder to the team members that this project was important.

- **Involvement**   Company-wide involvement was assured through the selection of team members from all relevant areas.

- **Leadership**   Credible team leadership was assured through selection as team leader of an experienced, successful branch manager, and situational leadership was encouraged through the assignment of tasks to individual team members.

- **Communication**   Timely communication was assured through the "accountability-based change management" process already in place, i.e., through the sponsor's regular reports back to the Executive Committee and through the project management software and real-time web site used by and visible to all team members.

- **Time & Resources**   Also, though it's not explicitly stated, the odds are good that—with the high-level sponsorship and the accountability procedures used—adequate time and resources were allocated to the project.

In the next chapter, some possible weaknesses in the Madison-Whyte example will be discussed.

Inside-Outside Perspective

When creating a team for a complex change, you may want to consider the advantages of an inside-outside team.

If you are an *internal* change agent, you may want to find an outside consultant to contribute expertise, support, and legitimacy to your efforts. Sometimes, organizational people listen better to outside experts (and sometimes they don't). And if you are that *outside* expert, you certainly will want to enlist an insider who understands the system, is supportive of the change and has some security and status.

As Havelock says, the point is "to maximize the strengths of both positions in the service of innovation." As you can see in the chart below (adapted from Havelock), each has advantages and disadvantages.

	ADVANTAGES	DISADVANTAGES
INSIDE	• knows the system • speaks the language • understands norms • identifies with the system • is familiar to adopters	• lacks perspective • lacks S/K • lacks power base • has past record • has existent role
OUTSIDE	• starts fresh • has perspective • is independent of structure • has relevant expertise	• is a stranger • lacks system knowledge • may not care enough

Developmental Stages of Teams

Like individual human beings, teams are created and—if all goes well—they develop. In *Team Players and Teamwork*, Glenn Parker elaborates on a team's four developmental stages.

FORM $\longrightarrow$ STORM $\longrightarrow$ NORM$\longrightarrow$ PERFORM

In the **forming** stage, team members assess the task to be done and take the measure of each other and their fit to the task. *What are we here for? Who are you?* This stage is similar to an infant's trying to get oriented to the world.

In the **storming** stage, team members often get into conflict with each other and with the leader as they resist the structure, assigned roles, even the task itself. *That's no way to do this. I have a much better idea.* This stage is similar to the rebelliousness of a young child toward the controls of parents and school.

In the **norming** stage, team members accept the task, each other, and whatever operating rules have evolved. They trust each other and share information. *We agree on what needs to be done. And how to do it.* This stage is similar to the socialization of the older child.

In the **performing** stage, team members are united and throw themselves into the task at hand. *Let's get to work. We can do this.* This stage is comparable to maturity in human development.

This is the theory as it relates to an *effective* team. However, in practice, a team may cycle several times through the stages or even get stuck at a stage. Understanding the stages and monitoring a team's progress can be helpful in two ways: you may be able to facilitate the team's development and you won't be surprised or offended if, after an initial agreeable beginning, they suddenly seem to be balking—storming. It's normal even for an effective team.

If You Want to Read More

Rogers' *Diffusion of Innovations*, Chapter 9, "The Change Agent" offers material not covered here. And Glenn Parker's *Team Players and Teamwork* goes into detail about various team roles as they are played out in each of the four developmental stages.

Skill Sets the
Change Team Needs

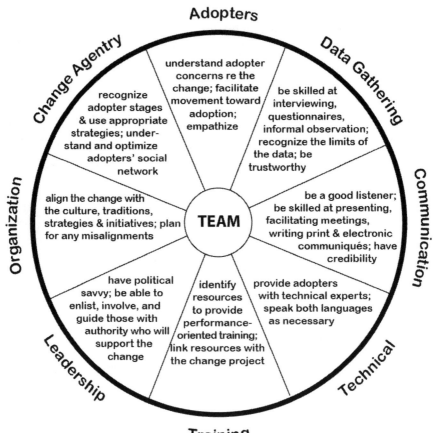

WORKSHEET 13 Assess your Change Team

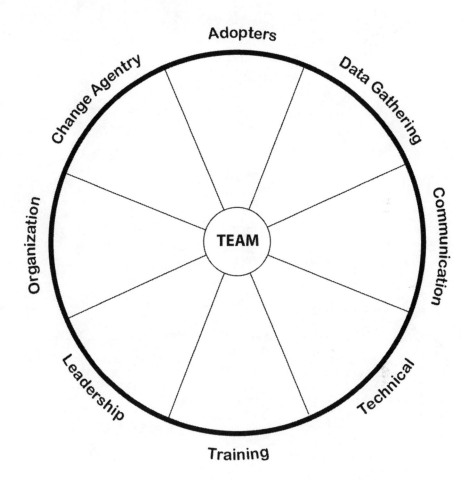

1. Record in each area of the Change Wheel the names of team members who are strong in that area. Some names may appear more than once. Indicate each person's potential contributions.

2. List areas that are weak or which have no name at all, as well as what you plan to do about it.

3. Revise or add to your Action Plan as necessary to reflect your Change Team's involvement.

10. Leadership & Participation

Leadership and participation, when viewed in the extreme, might be considered opposites. At the one extreme, a single decision-maker leads others through a process. At the other extreme, the entire group participates in the decision-making and other phases of the process. Before we look at how the two approaches might best play out in a change project, let's clarify what constitutes effective leadership and what constitutes effective participation. First, leadership.

Leadership

No one explains what leadership is—and what it is not—so well as Kotter does in *A Force for Change: How Leadership Differs From Management*. To begin with, he emphasizes that the phrase "leader of change" is redundant because the result of a successful leader is always a change. No change, no leadership! But what is leadership?

Kotter defines leadership by contrasting it with management. He sees the two as quite different, so different that they are sometimes in direct conflict. To begin with, they have *different goals*.

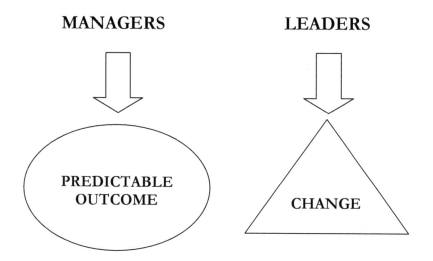

MANAGERS → PREDICTABLE OUTCOME

LEADERS → CHANGE

Managers have the goal of producing *predictable results* for stakeholders, e.g., making annual sales of $5 million, decreasing the percentage of high school dropouts, reducing insurance costs. In direct contrast, leaders have the goal of creating useful *change*, e.g., rejuvenating a company, turning a group of diverse soldiers into an effective army; making the society a more equitable place for all.

Management may or may not involve getting people to move in a given direction. Leadership always does! Consider Gloria Steinem, Martin Luther King, General George C. Patton, Magic Johnson, and Mahatma Gandhi.

In different situations and with different visions, each of them was able to rally people to their causes and get them moving toward a common goal. Their efforts resulted in change. They were leaders!

The following Change Aid summarizes Kotter's description of the *different tasks* and *skills* required for the two different roles.

Management vs. Leadership

(adapted from *A Force for Change* by John Kotter)

MANAGERS	LEADERS
Plan & Budget	**Set Direction**

Organize & Staff	**Align People**

Control & Problem-solve	**Motivate & Inspire**

**PREDICTABLE
OUTCOME**

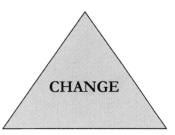

CHANGE

When you *manage*—with a clear goal in mind—you develop a plan and a budget to support your plan. Next, you create the organization and staff required to execute the plan. Then, you work to control unexpected and expected factors and to solve problems as they come up. *Change management involves all of these tasks and skills!*

When you *lead*, you have a clear vision and communicate it (set direction) to the people you want to move. Then, if the "battleship is really going to turn" in the desired direction, you identify and get the support of all relevant stakeholders (align people). Once the people are in motion, you involve, support and reward them (motivate and inspire), especially when the going gets tough. *Change management involves all of these tasks and skills!*

Change agents—like others—are usually more familiar with management skills, even when it's leadership skills that are needed. Therefore, let's look further at the three phrases of leadership.

The Three Phases of Leadership

Phase 1—Set Direction   Organizational people who succeed soon learn the initial management tasks of planning and budgeting. These are deductive processes that involve detailed documentation. Often, these same people do not learn the basic leadership skill—*setting direction*. In *Leaders*, Warren Bennis and Burt Nanus say,

> To choose a direction, a leader must first have developed a mental image of a possible and desirable future state of the organization. This image, which we call a vision, may be as vague as a dream or as precise as a goal or a mission statement. The critical point is that a vision articulates a view of a realistic, credible, attractive future for the organization, a condition that is better in some important ways than what now exists....A vision is a target that beckons.

To set direction, you begin with a broad range of information—much of it from targeted customers or potential adopters. You look for patterns and create a vision of the change that is specific enough to guide others, but open-ended enough to encourage initiative. You develop strategies to achieve the vision. Direction-setting is inductive and dynamic. (Jack Welch doodled his G.E. vision on a napkin.)

To set a direction—

- ### Be brief.
  Teddy Roosevelt: "Charge!"

- ### Use images that grab people.
  SAS: "We used to fly planes; now we fly people."

- ### Believe it—or forget it.
  Martin Luther King: "I have a dream that one day on the red hills of Georgia the sons of former slaves and the sons of former slave owners will be able to sit down together at the table of brotherhood."

Phase 2—Align People People who want to succeed in organizations soon learn the management tasks of organizing and staffing. These are design tasks that involve structures, jobs, compensation systems, types of staff needed. Often, these same people do not learn the basic leadership skill—*aligning people*. In *The Leadership Challenge*, James Kouzes and Barry Posner say,

> *The first task in enlisting others is to identify our constituents and find out what their common aspirations are. No matter how grand the dream of an individual visionary, if others don't see the possibility of realizing their own hopes and desires, they won't follow.*

To align people, you must be able to communicate so that people understand, relate, and care—an enormously challenging job. The audience is often diverse. The message is always new and usually complex. The message and the messenger must be credible and consistent. But, most important of all, you must present the change so that it relates—not so much to the organization—but to the concerns and needs of the targeted people.

To align people, see the change from *their* eyes—

The new process will increase shareholder value.	**No!**
The new process will make your job more secure.	**Yes!**
This technology will make the company competitive.	**No!**
This technology will make your job easier.	**Yes!**

Phase 3—Motivate & Inspire   People who want to succeed soon learn the management tasks of controlling relevant factors and solving problems. They know how to get people to comply with work standards and the business plan. Often, these same people do not learn the basic leadership skill—*motivating and inspiring people*. In *Reengineering the Corporation*, Michael Hammer and James Champy say,

> *We define a leader not as someone who makes other people do what he or she wants, but as someone who makes them want what he or she wants. A leader doesn't coerce people into change that they resist. A leader articulates a vision and persuades people that they want to become part of it, so that they willingly, even enthusiastically, accept the distress that accompanies its realization.*

To get people to achieve grand (or even modest) visions, overcome barriers and act with energy in the face of obstacles, you must motivate and inspire people. This kind of leadership task is almost diametrically opposed to the task of managing people. Managing involves controlling toward known results. Leading encourages movement toward the unknown—which is what turning a vision into reality always is. Leadership is bold! It brings about change!

To motivate and inspire, you communicate, involve, support, and reward—

ML is VP of Information Technology. She gets people to accept technological changes with little resistance. Why do they follow her lead?

The answers lie in what her employees say about her.

"She can be trusted. She's fair and tells you straight what she thinks. Even when she disagrees, she's respectful."

"She listens better than anyone I know."

"She's clear about what she's aiming for and what she wants you to aim for."

"She makes you feel like you belong to something."

"She helps you be more than you were."

Management *and* Leadership

A Change Project Needs Management   There is no doubt that a change project needs a lot of managing. Someone needs to plan and budget for the necessary communiqués, site visits, meetings, training. Someone needs to develop a budget, to figure out what staff is needed and to organize their efforts with a time and action calendar. Then, as the project goes along, someone needs to control things and solve problems as they come up. All of these tasks are aimed at getting "predictable results." But, that's just one side of what's needed.

A Change Project Needs Leadership If you want people to be involved and committed to the new way of doing things, you have to go beyond managing. First, someone needs to communicate a vision of how things can be. Then, someone has to get all of the people going in the same direction. And, when things go wrong or maybe just slower than expected and people get discouraged, someone has to motivate and inspire people to hang in.

Who Leads? Generally, change agents are primarily responsible for the management role, but they may also contribute leadership. As may some technical experts. However, leadership comes primarily from *sponsors* and *opinion leaders*.

An Example   The following examples of leadership are from a change project aimed at major cost-reductions through the use of new purchasing processes in a global company. First, leadership from a sponsor, then from an opinion leader, and finally from a member of the change team.

> **Leadership from a Sponsor**   *The sponsor of the cost-reduction project was the Director of Purchasing. He had a clear vision (reduce annual costs by $190 million). He was active in making public statements (presentation at annual purchasing conference) and private commitments (meetings with business unit managers) in support of the change. He allocated resources for special project assignments (travel funds for early users to become field coaches) and rewards (stock options).*

Leadership from an Opinion Leader *One of the targeted adopters, a buyer, had years of experience and the respect of his peers. He took on the task of developing a demonstration project using the new processes (consolidation of suppliers and aggressively negotiated contracts). Using the new system, he facilitated a win-win relationship with a major vendor, one that saved the company thousands of dollars. He gave a presentation on the pilot project's success at the annual purchasing conference.*

Leadership from Change Team Members *Members of the change team designed initial "vision" communiqués for clarity and high impact on the buyers targeted as users (adopters) of the new purchasing processes. Team members facilitated contacts between buyers and experienced users of the new processes. Team members arranged for the PR department to place success stories of local purchasing teams in local newspapers.*

As a change agent, you need all the leadership you can get from those who have *influence* (e.g., opinion leaders, technical experts, you and other members of the change team) and from those who have *authority* (e.g., sponsors and bosses). In earlier chapters, we looked at those with influence, now we'll look at those with authority.

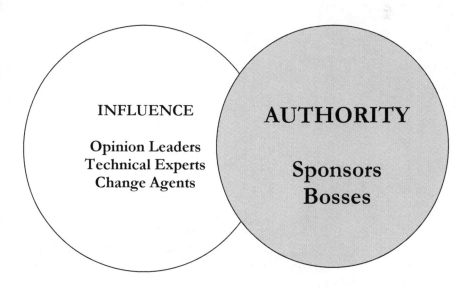

INFLUENCE

Opinion Leaders
Technical Experts
Change Agents

AUTHORITY

Sponsors
Bosses

Leaders with Authority

In a change project, the most powerful leadership comes from the authority system—most of all from the *sponsors* of the change.

Sponsors   What's a sponsor? (Some organizations refer to this role as a change *champion*.) A sponsor is a person or group with the *power and influence* to legitimize the change and to provide *continuing support*.

Usually, the sponsors are those who originally decided on the change. However, regardless of who made the decision, the change facilitator needs early on to figure out who the real *working* sponsors are. Who are those who are willing to lend their ongoing authority, resources, and time to the project? They are likely to be the most significant persons in any change effort.

In *Managing at the Speed of Change*, Daryl Conner describes a strong sponsor as one who

- ✓ believes a change will be useful and strongly advocates for it.
- ✓ has an in-depth understanding of the change and its long-range implications.
- ✓ accurately understands the size and scope of the target group.
- ✓ fully empathizes with what the target group is being asked to change.
- ✓ understands the resources—time, money, commitment, and people—which are needed and will commit them.
- ✓ is able and willing to demonstrate publicly both support and commitment.
- ✓ is able and willing to meet privately with key individuals or groups to convey strong personal support for the change.

The change facilitator's tasks here are to (1) identify the sponsors, (2) assess them for their understanding of and commitment to the change, and (3) help them give what is needed.

1. Identify the Sponsors First, determine who is behind the change. Even if there is one high-ranking decision-maker, there are often others of lower rank who are spearheading the change. You need sponsors who are not only powerful within the organization, but who will bring their power to bear on your change.

Try to get sponsors at the level you need. In general, the higher up in the organization, the better. However, to be cost-effective, active or working sponsorship is usually leveraged down to the lowest ranking person with the authority to make the change happen.

Leveraging Sponsorship

In a multinational company with 25 affiliates all over the globe, the CEO of the company may be the highest-level sponsor of a new company-wide quality program. But, for each of the affiliates to come aboard, the President of each affiliate is probably the highest level of "working" sponsorship. Even then, sponsorship may be leveraged down to the VPs and Executive Directors at each affiliate.

2. Assess Your Sponsors If at all possible, get sponsor data firsthand. Interview potential sponsors to find out what they see as the strengths and limitations of the change and what the level of their support is likely to be. Be sensitive to personal or political factors that may color their views and which they may express nonverbally or obliquely.

Try to see the change—its advantages and disadvantages—from their viewpoint. Once you feel like you have a good sense of where potential sponsors are coming from with regard to the change, it's time to rate them.

If you have more than one sponsor, make multiple copies of the next form. Don't just think about the answers, *fill in the form*. People often report that when they actually do this, they get some surprises and understand better what they're dealing with. After you've completed the form(s), continue reading.

WORKSHEET 14   Rate your sponsor.

Potential Sponsor_____

1. Specify what this person could provide. What do you want this person to do or say or give?

2. Rate this sponsor. How strong/weak is this person as a sponsor for this change? For each item, circle the number that best fits this person.

1 = not at all
2 = not much
3 = average
4 = somewhat
5 = totally

Does X really believe the change will be useful?   1 2 3 4 5

Does X really understand the change?   1 2 3 4 5

Does X empathize with what's ahead for the users? 1 2 3 4 5

Can X be counted on to commit needed resources? 1 2 3 4 5

Will X support the change with power & influence? 1 2 3 4 5

TOTAL

Sponsor Rating   If your total is 20 or above, you probably have a strong sponsor. If your total is below 15, you probably have a weak sponsor. Trouble may follow. If your total is below 10, and this is your major sponsor, failure is probable.

3. Manage this sponsor. Given the strengths and weaknesses of this sponsor, what must you do to get what's needed from this person?

Noted for his unvarnished way of stating things, Daryl Conner says that when sponsor commitment falls too low, the change facilitator has three options: (1) strengthen the sponsorship, (2) change sponsors, or (3) prepare to fail. Use this flowchart to assess your sponsor status.

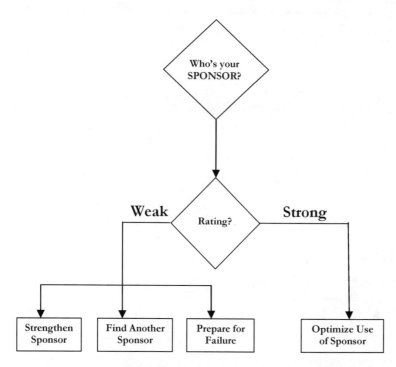

If you need to *strengthen a weak sponsor,* think of it as another change project. You want the person to make a change—to become an active, strong sponsor. Do an adopter analysis (i.e., look at the sponsor as the adopter of the role of sponsorship) and plan for the sponsor's stage of acceptance. What exactly would you like him/her to do? What stage is s/he in now? What can you do to facilitate progress to the next stage?

If you need to *find another sponsor,* that is easier said than done. If the sponsor is one of the good guys, but just doesn't have time, ask him/her for suggestions. If the sponsor is, for whatever reason, not so accessible and collaborative, you may have to stick with him/her. Good luck!

If you cannot find a sufficiently strong sponsor, you would do well to *plan your own survival* in the event of a failed change effort.

3. Help Your Sponsors   Even if you have a strong sponsor, you'll usually need to provide some help. Just because someone is a *willing* sponsor doesn't mean that they know how to be a *good* sponsor. It may be useful to review what the sponsor/leader is supposed to do so that you can help him/her do it at the right time. In *Leading Change*, Kotter proposes eight steps. Although he is aiming at large-scale change, these steps are also appropriate for the sponsor/leader of most smaller changes as well.

1.   Increase urgency
2.   Build the guiding team
3.   Get the vision right
4.   Communicate for buy-in
5.   Empower action
6.   Create short-term wins
7.   Don't let up
8.   Make change stick

You might use these as a check-list. Is it time for your sponsor to "increase urgency"? "build the guiding team? "get the vision right?" etc. Then, how can you help your sponsor do what's needed at the appropriate time?

One change facilitator referred to the support he gives his sponsors as their "homework." Here are some of the ways he helps:

✓ tentative brief list of sponsor tasks shared in early face-to-face meeting—to get agreement

✓ timely e-mail reminders of actions to take

✓ drafts of speeches for sponsor to present

✓ drafts of memos for sponsor to send

✓ timely e-mails re people to be contacted

✓ reminders of meeting agenda items to be covered

✓ brief interim reports to avoid surprises

Make it easy to be your project sponsor!

Bosses & the Chain of Authority   Although sponsors may be the most powerful authority figures you can have, certain bosses can intentionally or inadvertently help or destroy a change project. Hence, especially when the change agent and the adopters are not in the same organizational line of authority (and often they are not), it's important to identify every boss in between.

CHANGE AGENT

ADOPTERS

Who Are the Bosses That Matter? The bosses that matter are all of those in the organizational hierarchy who connect the change agents to the adopters. This constitutes a *chain of authority* for the change project.

People tend to do what their bosses view as important. Since it is not unusual for the responsibilities and requirements of an organizational change to get tacked onto both the adopters' and the change agent's regular jobs, it is even more important to get the bosses and the bosses' bosses aboard.

When these authority figures show that they value the change, adopters are more likely to cooperate, change agents are more likely to survive and the whole project is more likely to meet with success.

Some bosses may require little or no attention, but to ignore any boss is to invite problems, even disaster. Buy-in and appropriate action needs to reach as high as necessary to complete the chain of authority.

In the example below, as often happens, the change agent—the Training Director—is a staff person not in the direct line of authority over the adopters—the Branch Staff. This Director also has no authority over the three levels of managers over the branch staff.

In this case, the change agent needs to identify all bosses in the chain and keep them appropriately in the loop. In addition, he needs to get his own boss's input and approval of his plan to communicate with the other bosses. (Gray cells show the completed Chain of Authority)

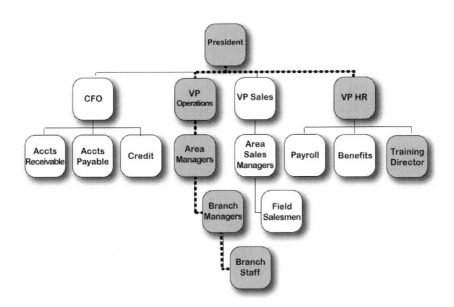

Once the highest authority has publicly endorsed the project, occasional update memos may be all that's needed. Other times, face-to-face meetings or more detailed reports may be called for. Don't overload them with information, but also—*never surprise a boss!* Don't let them find out from the rumor mill what's happening to their people.

What Can Bosses Do to Help?   Most bosses view management issues as the really important issues. They focus on getting predictable results. Some of what you need from them is, in fact, related to *management*. For example, they can offer insights on how the change will affect existent responsibilities and schedules, on the integration of change-related activities and regular work responsibilities and on resources.

But you can also use some *leadership* from the bosses relevant to your project. In fact, one of your jobs as a change agent is to help bosses do a bit of leading for your change. For example, they can offer legitimacy for making project-related activities part of adopters' or change team member's jobs, rewards for adopters who buy into the change, rewards for change team members for project successes.

Use high-level supporters sparingly. They can be your trump card, useful for high impact at crucial times.

Make it easy for them to help. High-level people are usually spread thin. Protect their time and effort.

Have a contingency plan. High-level people are always moving on— to another project, responsibility, job, or even organization. Be ready in case your best power players leave.

High-level supporters are hard to get.

High-level supporters are hard to keep.

Take good care of them!

WORKSHEET 15   Draw an organizational chart and indicate all relevant people, their titles, and their roles in your change project.

Participation

Remember the study on worker rewards? According to the workers, one of the top three most-valued rewards was a feeling of "being in on things." People like to have control over their lives. One way for them to have some control is to participate in any process that will involve or affect them. Moreover, end-users usually know more about their situation than anyone else, so getting them involved can improve the result. Of course, such participation means that at least some of the decision-making, some of the power will be in their hands. *Power to the People?* Can the people really be trusted with power? Some of the experts think so.

For example, in *The Inmates Are Running the Asylum,* Alan Cooper makes the case for shifting decision-making for technology design from the designers to the users. In *User Design,* Allison Carr-Chellman makes the case for shifting the decision-making for instructional design from the designers and teachers to the learners. Dozens of empowerment books make the case for shifting the decision-making for organizational tasks to the workers. So, what's this got to do with change agentry? How far should change agents and high-level decision makers go in empowering targeted users to participate in change efforts? First, let's look at two examples of how a change might be approached.

Example—The Usual Way Jeanne Duck described one way changes are approached. (Referred to earlier, her scenario is paraphrased here.)

> *The CEO announces that changes are needed and appoints a task force to come up with a design. He orders them to report back to him in 90 days.*

> *The task force shuts itself away in a meeting room and puts in long hours to meet the CEO's deadline. They agree that telling others what they're doing would only slow them down and, besides, they'll make an announcement when they're ready. They assume that, until then, no one knows what they're doing.*

"But," Duck says, "the opposite is true. Everything that is or is not done sends a message."

When the CEO announced that changes were needed and appointed the task force, everyone knew that something was up. And they knew that they weren't "in on things." In the absence of information, people horribilize and rumors fly.

The secrecy of the task force has prevented the targeted users from "participating or buying in."

Example—A Better Way   The earlier Madison-Whyte case about a new pricing system offered a different picture of the change process. Members of the task force (change team) were selected from relevant areas of the company.

An 11-member change team (or task force) was created with representatives from every group that would be affected by the change. The adopters were represented by four of their managers. The manager of the top-performing branch was appointed the formal leader of the team. Having the VP who was sponsoring the change as a participating member was an unusual, added advantage.

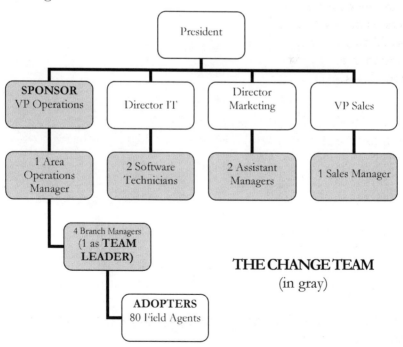

This case was presented as an example of effective sponsorship, widespread involvement, leadership, communication and accountability and, indeed, it was, but were there weaknesses also?

From the information given, it seems likely that, although there was widespread involvement, *end-users* (the 80 field agents who had been overriding prices) *were not involved* in any part of this project. They seem to have first found out that they could no longer override prices when they tried to enter prices into the computer and were locked out. This is not the ideal way for a worker to learn that he himself has been overridden. Unfortunately, it is not unusual for higher levels in an organization to forget to involve the lowest level workers in their change planning. It also appears that, at Madison-Whyte, *only top management defines problems.* This not only works against buy-in from lower-level employees, but it reduces the probability that those problems known only by the front line workers will get attention.

However, the facts are not so gloomy! What was not told in the earlier description is that, prior to the development of the Pricing Task Force, some other things had happened.

At an earlier Executive Committee meeting, the pricing problem had been only one of a number of company-wide problems that were addressed. The other problems had been identified through an anonymous survey which had been sent to every employee in the company. The results had been tabulated company-wide and also by individual branches. Although members of the Executive Committee gave the pricing problem the top priority, they also addressed the problems identified by the employees.

Subsequently, the President, with an assistant, scheduled meetings at each of the 34 branches. All employees were requested to attend and compensated for their time. The President made a brief presentation noting the major company-wide problems and the major local problems identified by the employees. He also described the pricing problem and the task force addressing it. After the President's presentation, he opened the meeting up and encouraged employees to react and offer suggestions. He wrapped the meeting up by telling them what they could expect next and also by asking the field agents, in particular, to channel any suggestions they might have to one of the members of the Pricing Task Force.

So, although the field agents would not be directly involved in the pricing system design, they had been informed about the change in a situation in which employee concerns had been addressed and they had been given a way to input to the process.

Centralized and Decentralized Approaches   The two preceding examples illustrate the difference between what Rogers calls a centralized and a decentralized approach to change. He defines the centralized approach as a "linear, one-way model of communication" in which the change "originates from some expert source" and is diffused to the adopters as a package which they passively accept or not. He contrasts this approach with a decentralized system and defines it as one "in which participants create and share information with one another in order to reach a mutual understanding" and in which the changes

> ...*often bubble up from operational levels of a system, with the inventing done by lead users. Then the ideas spread horizontally via peer networks, with a high degree of re-invention occurring as the innovations are modified by users to fit their particular conditions....decision making ...is widely shared, with adopters making many decisions.*

Rogers cautions that the decentralized type of system is most effective when

> *(1) the users are highly educated and technically competent practitioners (for example, cardiovascular surgeons), so that all the users are experts, or (2) the innovations being diffused do not involve a sophisticated level of technology (for example, home energy conservation or organic gardening versus building a nuclear power plant), so that intelligent laymen have sufficient technical expertise to take advantage of them.*

This is compatible with the suggestion made earlier that, if the adopters are to make adaptations to the change itself (and they don't have to be cardiovascular surgeons unless they're doing cardiovascular surgery), it is important that they not destroy its critical functions or integrity. In other words: *If users are going to make design decisions, they should know what they're doing!* But don't underestimate their expertise!

Also, design is not the only—and often not the most realistic—way adopters can be involved in a change project. *They can almost always have a say in the implementation phase.* What adjustments in the current job situation will need to be made? How will the change affect other jobs in the workplace? What timeline makes the most sense? Users know more about their work situation than others do

Rosabeth Moss Kanter wrote this about involving people:

> **"Change is a threat when done to me, but an opportunity when done by me."** *I coined this truth in my book* The Change Masters. . . *Resistance is always greatest when change is inflicted on people without their involvement, making the change effort feel oppressive or constraining. If it is possible to tie change to things people already want, and give them a chance to act on their own goals and aspirations, then it is met with more enthusiasm and commitment.*

It is reasonable to suggest that end-users should have as much involvement and responsibility as it is possible and practical for them to have—whether in the design of the change or in its implementation. Ask yourself—What can they do? Where can they contribute? What would I want if I were in their shoes?

If you find yourself (or your sponsor) thinking, "Wait a minute! We don't have time for all those people to get involved in this project," you don't have to involve everyone on every change project, but you would do well to identify and involve significant people in the adopter group who may cause trouble later. Remember what Daryl Conner says, "Pay now, or pay later!"

Leadership *and* Participation

Setting leadership and participation up as opposites, as I did at the beginning of this chapter, is obviously a straw man. It isn't an either-or situation. Change projects need both. They need effective *leadership* from sponsors, bosses, opinion leaders, technical experts and members of the change team. They need appropriate *participation* by adopters and other stakeholders.

WORKSHEET 16 Revisit your Action Plan.

1. Stage-by-stage, list (in the last column of your Action Plan) the actions you want/need from your leaders, e.g. sponsors, bosses, opinion leaders, change team, others.

2. Stage-by-stage, add any ways not already noted that your adopters or others might participate in the change process.

If You Want to Read More

Daryl Conner's *Managing at the Speed of Change* is easy to read and likely to leave you with valuable insights and principles you won't forget. (Given my frequent mention of him in this book, you can see that I didn't forget.)

Almost all of John Kotter's books offer the change agent something of value. One of his earliest, *Power and Influence,* gives mid-level organizational people useful guidance about how to have influence even though they have little or no authority.

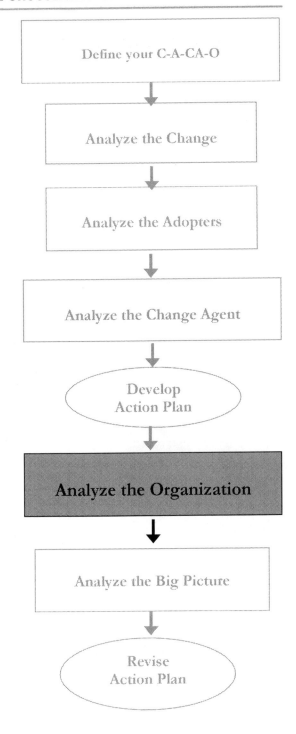

11. The **ORGANIZATION**

Changes, adopters, and change agents do not exist in isolation. They exist within an *organizational context.*

This context includes the *culture, image, guidelines, technologies, change climate* and certain *people*—all of which can have an impact on your change project. The big question is...

How well does your change project align with its organizational context?

Culture

How important is the organization's culture? Many experts suggest that change efforts are doomed if they are in conflict with the prevailing culture of the organization. Kim Cameron and Robert Quinn say, "The failure rate of most planned organizational change initiatives is dramatic...Several studies reported that the most frequently cited reason given for failure was a neglect of the organization's culture." Daryl Conner says, "The magnitude of cultural impact on a change effort is massive. In fact, significant change will only be sustained when supported by an organization's culture." Lou Gerstner, the former CEO of IBM, says, "Culture isn't just one aspect of the game—it *is* the game."

What is culture? Terrence Deal and Allan Kennedy propose the most succinct definition—*It's the way things get done around here.* Cameron and Quinn elaborate,

> *...it encompasses the taken-for-granted values, underlying assumptions, expectations, collective memories, and definitions present in an organization...It reflects the prevailing ideology that people carry inside their heads. It conveys a sense of identity to employees, provides unwritten and often unspoken guidelines for how to get along in the organization, and it enhances the stability of the social system that they experience.*

Can you change the culture? The experts disagree somewhat about whether or not you can change the culture. On the one hand, Schein asks, "Can you imagine saying that the United States, or France, needs a new culture?" On the other hand, Cameron and Quinn are among those who offer ways to change the culture. However, culture change efforts require broad-based commitment and are likely to take years. Hence, with the kind of changes for which mid-level people are responsible, it's probably wise to hold the view—*If your change doesn't align with the organization's culture, get ready to modify your change. Or to fail.*

How can you understand the culture? One problem for internal change agents is that they live and work inside the culture, take it for granted and, hence, may have a hard time seeing what it is. However, even internal change agents can use various assessment approaches and tools to understand the culture.

Gareth Morgan describes one approach to assessment,

> *One of the easiest ways of appreciating the nature of culture and subculture is simply to observe the day-to-day functioning of a group or organization to which one belongs, as if one were an outsider. Adopt the role of anthropologist. The characteristics of the culture being observed will gradually become evident as one becomes aware of the patterns of interaction between individuals, the language that is used, the images and themes explored in conversation, and the various rituals of daily routine.*

Edgar Schein begins with the same anthropological approach, but adds the concept of three levels, with each level taking you deeper into an understanding of the culture. Each level requires more skill and effort to de-code and interpret.

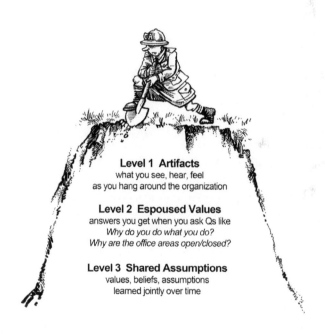

Level 1 Artifacts
what you see, hear, feel
as you hang around the organization

Level 2 Espoused Values
answers you get when you ask Qs like
Why do you do what you do?
Why are the office areas open/closed?

Level 3 Shared Assumptions
values, beliefs, assumptions
learned jointly over time

Schein cautions that while it may be relatively easy to identify the "artifacts" of an organization (e.g., the way people dress, speak and interact; the way space is used; who eats with whom), it requires an in-depth study to identify the "shared assumptions" people have. He emphasizes that it is those assumptions which most affect the effort to introduce change.

In *The Corporate Culture Survival Guide*, Schein details a method of assessment based on his three levels and includes both standard questions (e.g., What is the mission?) and unique ones. Here are some of his more unusual questions to whet your appetite:

Does your organization use special jargon or acronyms that you take for granted?

If teamwork is espoused, how does it work out in practice?

How does the physical layout reflect working style and status?

In your work situation, what do you consider to be a reward or a punishment?

How appropriate is it to interrupt the boss when he or she is speaking?

If you have to go home, say, to tend to a child, do you feel comfortable explaining the situation?

Especially when you are trying to understand the culture of your own organization, such questions can give you a new perspective and help you function like the recommended anthropologist.

A more structured approach is offered by Cameron and Quinn with their validated tool—the Organizational Culture Assessment Instrument (OCAI). It is not only relatively straightforward to use but it can also be an effective team builder and serve to facilitate change. (See End Notes.)

Multiple Cultures It's important to note that when the organization is large enough, the culture of one area may differ from the culture of another. One example is the common difference between the culture of an R & D unit and that of a marketing unit in the same corporation. Another example is offered by Conner. He had been consulting in a government agency during the Democratic administration. The day after Reagan's election, he said to his client, "Well, I guess a lot of things will change here now." The client chuckled and said, "It will be years before what's going on in the White House trickles down to us."

WORKSHEET 17   Be an anthropologist. Do a culture assessment. (If you want to do a more in-depth assessment, you may want to get *Diagnosing and Changing Organizational Culture* by Cameron and Quinn. Their validated instrument is relatively easy to use and interpret.)

1. Walk around, trying to see things with the eyes of a stranger. Pay attention to such things as...

- look and feel of the place
- dress (formal? informal? stated dress code?)
- dining areas (any special ones?)
- symbols
- ways of behaving, talking

Write about what you saw.

2. In writing, describe in a few words...

- schedules (e.g., flexible, fixed)
- meeting routines (e.g., frequency, way they're run, on time)
- rituals, social events
- way you find out things
- way conflicts are handled
- performance evaluations

3. Write your answers to these questions.

- Are there inconsistencies between publicly stated values, etc. and actual behaviors and practices?
- How is this organization different from others you have known?
- Are there special privileges for some?
- Is it okay to disagree with the boss? in front of others?
- Can you share personal problems with your boss? your colleagues?
- How are people rewarded or punished for performance?

Image

As Schein pointed out, there are various indicators of organizational culture. Most of us have learned to associate certain images with certain indicators. For example, if you hear someone say, "That office operates like a machine!" you assume that the employees are highly regulated and lack the freedom to innovate. Or if you hear, "That place is a jungle!" you assume that the employees engage in a lot of in-fighting over who gets what. "Machine" and "jungle" are just two of the images theorists have proposed to describe an organization.

In *Images of Organization*, Gareth Morgan says,

> *Effective managers and professionals in all walks of life...have to become skilled in the art of 'reading' the situations that they are attempting to organize or manage...Skilled readers develop the knack of reading situations with various scenarios in mind, and of forging actions that seem appropriate to the readings thus obtained... many of our conventional ideas about organization and management build on a small number of taken-for-granted images...*

Morgan describes eight images and suggests there are others. Another theorist, Joan Gallos, proposes four. (See End Notes for more details.) Taking the work of these two theorists into consideration along with my own judgment about which images may be most useful to the practitioner, the Chocolate Model proposes these four: *machine, brain, political,* and *family*.

EXERCISE   Before reading further, jot down which of the four images—machine, brain, political, family—you think might be dominant in each of these organizations.

university

fast-food restaurant

YMCA

high-tech company

Machine Image

You probably had no trouble choosing the *machine image* as the match for a fast-food restaurant, e.g., McDonald's. Everything is standardized—ingredients, cooking times, how high the coffee cups are filled, what the workers do and say to customers, etc.

The assumptions underlying an organization that operates according to the machine image include these:

- rational approaches are best

- performance is highest when people specialize

- personnel must be tightly controlled

- structure must align with organizational goals, tasks, technology and environment

- to fix problems, re-structure and create mechanisms to coordinate individual, group and unit efforts

While most organizations in the 19th and early 20th centuries fit the machine image (e.g., Henry Ford's mass-production line or Charlie Chaplin's factory in the classic film, *Modern Times*) there are also many current examples: assembly plants, telemarketers with job aids, technical help desks in Bangalore, waitresses who greet you in the voice of a cheerful robot, "My name is Clarice. I'll be your server tonight." (Note that Clarice may need to give this ritualized speech in order to keep her job but, in order to get large tips, she has to communicate that neither she nor you are parts of the machine.)

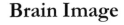

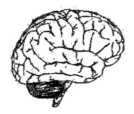

You may also have found it easy to pair up the *brain image* with high-tech companies.

The assumptions underlying an organization that operates according to the brain image include these:

- organizations are information-processing systems
- everything is open to inquiry and criticism
- learning, self-organization, and change are expected
- strategy is based on the avoidance of negative consequences and waste
- collaborative idea-generation is encouraged

The brain image is especially appropriate for R&D departments where discovery, innovation and creativity are essential. It is also appropriate for an entire company during the start-up period. Apple is a good example.

When Apple was new, rules and regulations were hard to find. Employees interacted as they saw fit to explore new ideas and develop new products. Later, after the company became highly successful, things changed. Accountability became the order of the day and a new, different kind of CEO was hired. Later, Steve Jobs again became CEO and he re-established "skunk works" which again operated in the brain image—safely away from the mainstream of the business, even having a building of their own.

Political Image

You may be surprised to find that a university is a good example of the *political image.*

The essence of the political image is that the organization exists as a coalition among groups with *different interests* in a condition of *scarce resources* for which they must compete. Consider a university-wide budget meeting in tough economic times attended by deans responsible for the sciences, the music school and the athletic program. Do they have different interests? You bet. Do they compete for funds? You better believe they do.

The assumptions underlying an organization that operates according to the political image include these:

- organizations are coalitions of individuals and interest groups

- members have different values, beliefs, interests, world views

- important decisions involve who gets what

- scarce resources make conflict inevitable

- power is a key asset

All organizations probably have some element of politics, whether that organization is a family with the children competing for their parent's time, a local city council with representatives competing for neighborhood sidewalks, a global manufacturing corporation with plant managers competing for budgets, or the U.S. Congress with representatives from the states competing for everything.

Family Image

You probably aren't surprised to find that YMCAs are good examples of the *family image*. After all, their stated reason for existing is to promote positive personal growth and relationships among their staff, their members, and the community.

The assumptions underlying an organization that operates according to the family image include these:

- organizations exist to serve human needs
- people and organizations need each other
- if the fit between the people and the organization is poor, both suffer
- if the fit is good, both prosper
- to fix problems, revise the organization to fit people needs and/or train individuals to meet organizational needs

The family image of an organization derives from the work of such theorists as Abraham Maslow, a humanistic psychologist. Joan Gallos says that the family image "captures the symbiotic relationship between individuals and organizations: individuals need opportunities to express their talents and skills; organizations need human energy and contribution to fuel their effort."

Non-profits, in particular, tend to operate according to the family image.

Multiple Images As you've seen, one image is often dominant in an organization or a part of it. The military might seem to be the quintessential example of a one-image organization, that of the machine. This is not surprising if you know the history of armies.

Frederick the Great's Army

Throughout history, armies had just been hordes of miscellaneous men running this way and that over the battlefield. But in the 18th century, Frederick the Great of Prussia changed all that.

Frederick was fascinated by automated toys like mechanical men and he began to think about creating a "mechanical" army, one with regulations, a command language, assigned ranks, uniforms. Systematic training would allow the parts to be created from almost any raw material and make it easy to replace them. The men would fear their officers more than the enemy, hence insuring that they would fight on command.

Frederick's army and, for many years, those that followed were almost pure examples of the machine image. In modern times, however, things have changed. Consider the contemporary military. It includes examples of all four images.

Machine On the battlefield, the formal chain of command, policies and procedures are crucial.

Family The number one asset is people. Hence, they get training, they're helped to get an education and mentoring is available to help them develop in all areas of their lives.

Brain All branches have think tanks and research branches. They are always trying to be better at what they do.

Political Each of the Joint Chiefs of Staff has a different set of interests and competes for limited resources.

This example is intended as a reminder that, while the concept of mental images can help you understand the organization you work in, it is important not to get trapped in a stereotype. Even McDonald's shows evidence of a brain image at the top.

Guidelines

Along with the culture, the organization's stated *guidelines* can have an impact on your change project. After all, existent guidelines—mission, strategies, policies and procedures, initiatives—are in place to steer the organization and its people. They tell, not only *why* the organization exists, but *how* to do the organizational tasks. When your change is aligned with them, you have potential support (although you may need to make the alignment visible to activate that support). When your change is not aligned, you need to recognize that and plan accordingly.

Mission   The most basic guideline is the mission. It answers the question—*Why* does the organization exist? At its most functional, everyone in the organization knows and lives the mission. Here's an example of how effective a mission statement can be.

Every effort counts!

Back in the 60s, a group of US Senators were visiting NASA at the time when funding was under threat. One Senator asked a man who was cleaning the floor, "So what are you doing here?"

The man answered, "I'm putting a man on the Moon!"

Strategy   In simple terms, strategy answers the question—*How* can the organization achieve its mission? Parish et al. concluded that

> *...organization leaders must strive to demonstrate to employees how any change implementation fits with the firm's larger strategic picture. Employees who understand that congruence are more likely to be committed to the change...*

Policies & Procedures   *Policies tend to be general* and broadly connect the organization's operations to its mission. *Procedures are specific.* They provide details, even step-by-step instructions, on how to implement policies. Taken together, policies and procedures regulate daily operations, inform employees as to their roles and responsibilities, and provide accountability.

Change agents need to identify early any misalignment between the change and the organization's policies and procedures. When the change requires modification of *procedures*—and it often does—this should be foreseen and planned for. However, when the change is at odds with a *policy*, the situation is more challenging. The change agent may then need the active support of higher level management. Or, as Conner might say, prepare to fail.

Initiatives   In many organizations, top-level managers meet annually to identify a few major objectives for the coming year. For the best-run organizations, these are carefully thought-out and important. For others, the process is more ritualistic than meaningful. However, in both cases, when the change is compatible with the initiatives, the change agent may be able to get some mileage out of making this compatibility evident.

In Sum   The point here is that, if you can piggy-back on existent guidelines—mission, strategies, policies, procedures, initiatives—you may be able to make a strong argument for your change. If, by contrast, your change is at odds with existent guidelines, you may be headed for trouble unless you enlist high-level support and/or modify the change to be in alignment.

Technologies

The term "technology" can be used to mean a wide range of skills, knowledge, machinery, or tools, but, in today's workplace, the most common use has to do with information or electronic technologies. Whether electronic or otherwise, technologies are so pervasive in today's organizations that it is almost certain that some of them will impact your change project. (In fact, one or more of them may actually be your change.) It's up to you to figure out which ones are likely to matter and to take them into consideration in your planning.

Change Climate

An organization may be generally open or closed to change. An open climate is characterized by flexibility, mutual respect, low threat and a sense of group membership. The communication flow, decision-making procedures and reward system are conducive to change. Obviously, the general change climate is related to the image from which the organization operates. A machine kind of organization is not likely to be open to change except on a limited basis and only from above. By contrast, a brain kind of organization depends on change. What kind of change climate does your organization have?

Change Load

Regardless of whether the organization is *generally* open or closed to change, the *current* change load can be a significant factor in any change effort. How many changes have the adopters had to deal with in the recent past? How many of these have brought real improvements for the adopters?

As you saw in the earlier Stress Test, people can take only so much change before they stop being functional. If your targeted adopters are already crushed by the load of change, you might suggest postponing the change. In any event, you may need to provide stress-reducing techniques (some of which are offered in the last chapter).

WORKSHEET 18   Analyze the organizational context of your change.

1. Image   Which of the four images is most prevalent in your organization and/or in your adopters' part of the organization? How so?

2. Guidelines

- What is the mission?
- What are the major strategies?
- What policies and/or procedures may relate to your change?
- What current initiatives exist?

Are any of these likely to impact on or be impacted by your change project?

3. Technologies   What technologies are likely to impact on or be impacted by your change?

4. Change Climate   Is your organization or the adopters' part of it open or closed to change?

5. Change Load   Are your adopters overloaded with change? How so? If they are, what can you plan that might help?

Alignment

When your change fits with the current status of the organization, your chance of success as a change agent is increased. When it doesn't fit, you may be in for trouble. In either case, you can plan accordingly, either taking full advantage of alignment, modifying your change to be better aligned, or preparing for the outcome of misalignment.

WORKSHEET 19   Rate your change's alignment with its organizational context.

5 = totally aligned
4 = mostly aligned
3 = half-aligned, half-misaligned
2 = mostly misaligned
1 = totally misaligned

1. culture   _____

2. image   _____

3. mission   _____

4. strategy   _____

5. policies & procedures   _____

6. current initiatives   _____

7. technologies   _____

8. change climate   _____

9. change load   _____

TOTAL

If you got a total of 45, you're in terrific alignment with your organization, a benefit of which you can take advantage of throughout the project. If a total of 9, you may need to look for another job or, at least, another project. A total of 27 or less should sound an alarm, as should any item with a rating of 3 or less.

People

Insofar as a change project goes, we've already looked at the most important organizational people—adopters, sponsors, bosses, and change agents. However, there are a few others to consider. These include *gatekeepers, informal networks,* and those with *special interests.*

Gatekeepers

Gatekeepers are those people who can give or withhold information or access. For example, an administrative assistant can keep you from getting an appointment. An IT clerk can delay the figures necessary for a new system. The custodian can lock the meeting room door and disappear. It pays to identify and nurture those who guard the gates.

Informal Networks

Once you've identified those who are critical to your adoption efforts (e.g., sponsors, bosses, opinion leaders, innovators), you may benefit by looking at their *informal networks.* With whom do they eat lunch? jog? date? Earlier, Kirkpatrick's list of things you should know was mentioned, along with the difficulty of asking such questions. However, it often only takes asking *yourself.* Once you focus on the question, you may find that you already know the answer.

The reason for doing this is not because you're practicing to become a private eye who digs into people's personal lives, but because, as a change agent, *you need to know how information flows among the people who matter.* Even when you know what to say and when to say it, it helps to know to whom to say it and where it will be passed on.

Special Interest People

Each change project may involve people who have special interests. These might include the designers of the change, the consultants who proposed it, the vendors who sold it, or any others who have a stake in its success or failure. It's worthwhile to account for all stakeholders.

WORKSHEET 20   Note any additional people you should take into consideration and what you should know or do about them.

Gatekeepers
Informal Networks
Special Interest People

If You Want to Read More

Gareth Morgan is a scholar who—with *Images of Organization*—has written a book that is likely to change forever the way you think about and understand organizations. Not for the weak-of-heart reader, but—even if you get through only a few of his images—it's worth the effort.

I also recommend Edgar Schein's *The Corporate Culture Survival Guide*. The first part is especially relevant to change management.

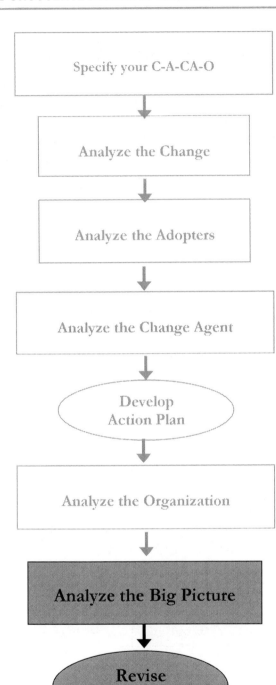

12. The Big Picture

You may not have been aware of it but, as you've moved through the Chocolate Model process, you've taken a bigger and bigger perspective. At the beginning, you looked at individual adopters, then at the adopter group, then at the organization and its relevant dimensions and people. Now you're going to get an even broader perspective. First, by looking at the *external influences* that may come from outside the organization to impact on your change. Then, by looking at the entire *change project system*. Finally, by developing a *Balance Sheet* for assessing all dimensions of the change project.

External Influences

External influences include all of the factors coming from outside of the organization that may impact on a given change project within the organization. Here are some:

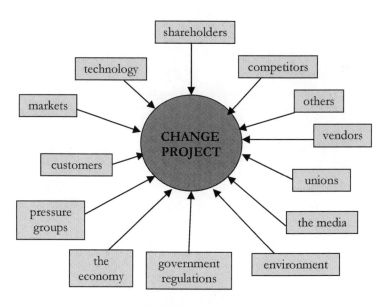

Sometimes, the best intentioned change effort can be done in by unexpected external influences, as is illustrated in the next example.

Goodwin's Was 150 Years Old

In the mid-80s, Goodwin's was the main distributor for plumbing supplies in a five county region. They had been in business for 150 years. But times were changing and Goodwin's management decided to computerize. They bought an integrated inventory/accounting system from a long-established computer company. The new system hadn't been installed long when it became evident that is was unreliable. Inventories came and went. One month all accounts receivable evaporated and only those customers who knew what they owed and were honest paid their bills.

The computer company sent consultants who introduced patch after patch—to no avail. Finally they took the problem to their own development engineers. No solution! This went on for 1½ years. Near the end of this period, some of the consultants took pity on Goodwin's and shared some internal documents which showed that the computer company had known all along that the system was dysfunctional and had asked their consultants to "buy time any way you can." At that point, Goodwin's sued for fraud and the case went to the county courts.

Things looked up! With all the evidence Goodwin's had, they felt certain they could win and get a large enough settlement to save the company. Then, a recession hit and business dropped off. The combination of the chaos caused by the faulty system and the decline in sales forced Goodwin to file for bankruptcy in the state court.

But, according to the law, once a company has filed for bankruptcy, the debtors are required to work through the state court, and the state court takes precedent over the county court even though the state case is a civil action and county case is a criminal action. Therefore, the state judge is the ultimate decision maker. Before the case could come to trial in the county court, the state judge decided that, if the computer company would settle with Goodwin's debtors, he would override any action by the county court and the bankruptcy would be finalized. Goodwin's got nothing. After 150 years, the oldest business in town closed its doors.

Goodwin was done in by three unexpected and unrelated external influences. The first was an *unreliable vendor* that sold the company a computerized system that disrupted their established processes without replacing them with automated processes that worked. The second was a national economic *recession*. The third was a *legal decision*.

WORKSHEET 21   Check the external influences that may impact your change project. Then, on the right, note exactly what that external influence is and what its relationship and influence are likely to be. (If your project is in a not-for-profit, you may need to modify the items. For example, you may not have shareholders, but rather a board of directors.)

✓	EXTERNAL INFLUENCE
	Shareholders
	Markets
	Customers
	Economy
	Technology
	Competitors
	Gov't Regulations
	Unions
	Vendors
	Pressure Groups
	The Media
	Environment
	Other

Unintended Consequences   Could any of the external influences that did Goodwin's in have been identified ahead of time? Perhaps, if a Unexpected Consequences Analysis had been done. Such an analysis is always a good idea before the change project has gone too far.

Here's an example of a change, the unexpected consequences of which were significant and which might have been foreseen if someone had asked the right questions.

It's Safe Here!

Safe Haven Laws, which decriminalize the act of leaving unharmed children to be cared for by the state, are intended as an alternative to the abortion, abandonment, or murder of infants by parents who do not want them. In July 2008, Nebraska became the last state in the union to pass such a law.

One day a few months later, three fathers walked into two Omaha hospitals and left their children. One left nine children, ages 1 to 17. Before the law was revised in November, 36 children had been left in Nebraska hospitals. None were infants.

Definitely an unintended consequence!

The original Nebraska law failed to include an age limit. Needless to say, the law was revised and now allows only for infants up to 30 days old.

WORKSHEET 22   Do an unintended consequence analysis. (There's added value in doing this with a team.) What could go wrong? What's the worst thing that could happen during this project? to the project? to you? to your team? If it does, what back-up plan might you have?

Change Project System

One thing to learn from the example of the 150 year old company is that a *systems* view can make a positive difference in the successful planning and implementing of a change project. Earlier you looked at the social system of the adopters and electronic networks, but it's possible to take a systems view of many things. First, what is a systems view? What is a system?

What Is a System?   One definition of a system is "a communicating network with a purpose." Some systems are information and control technologies. Wal-Mart's computerized warehouse software is a good example of a systems approach:

> *Wal-Mart invented the practice of sharing sales data via computer with major suppliers, such as Proctor & Gamble. Every time a box of Tide is rung up at the cash register, Wal-Mart's data warehouse takes note and knows when it is time to alert P&G to replenish a particular store. As a result, Wal-Mart stores rarely run out of stock of popular items.*

Imagine that "communicating network." Seven thousand Wal-mart stores connected with suppliers across the nation, all "with the purpose" of keeping every shelf in every store stocked. Wow! What a system!

We live in a world of systems. Like Wal-Mart's warehouse system, some are technical—electronic information systems, transportation systems, air controller systems. Some are not so technical—family household maintenance systems, carpool systems. Some are natural—the human digestive system, the solar system. *Some systems are technical; some are not.*

But whatever kind of system it is, it will be affected by the introduction of a "foreign object." For example, the introduction of a power outage has an effect on an electronic system, the introduction of a traffic jam has an effect on a carpool system, and the introduction of food has an effect on the human body. *Foreign objects have an effect on systems.*

Some foreign bodies make the system work better and some disrupt or even destroy the system. For example, when gasoline is introduced into the fuel system of a car, the car runs, but when water is introduced into the fuel system, the car stops. When food or a metal joint replacement is introduced into the human body, it has a good effect; when poison or a bullet is introduced, it has a bad effect. *The effect of foreign objects can be good or bad.*

The effect can work in the opposite direction too. The body is not only affected by foreign objects, it affects the foreign objects. For example, the body *converts* some foreign objects—water, food, medicine—and the body *ejects* some foreign objects—poison that is regurgitated, an implanted organ that is rejected. *Not only does a foreign object affect the system, but the system affects the foreign object.*

In sum,

- Some systems are technical, some are not.

- A foreign object affects—for good or bad—the system.

- The system affects—for good or bad—the foreign object.

What, you may ask, does this have to do with a change project? Look at it this way—the organization and the people who work in it are going along in a certain way. They exist and work within one or more systems. Then someone introduces a "foreign body"—a change. Whether or not it turns out to be for the good—*The change affects the way the systems work. The systems affect the way the change works.*

Here's an example from a consultancy of mine (names changed).

The Med-Am Case

Brooks Hospital, the largest, most successful hospital in the state financed a spin-off corporation—Med-Am Programs Inc. The new corporation's mission was to franchise specialty medical programs throughout the nation. The strategy was to target hospitals in their home state first. Since Brooks' Pain Treatment Program had been both a treatment and a financial success, it was selected as the first to be offered.

Med-Am was well-financed with a small, top-heavy staff—a President, Vice-President of Finance, Vice-President of Programs and a secretary. Although the three officers were capable at marketing and sales, they recognized that, once a sale was made, they would need help to replicate the existing program for the new hospital. Med-Am's President had attended one of my workshops so he called me.

After doing an on-site analysis of Brooks Pain Program, I developed a plan for a two-week training program and got approval from the client. When Med-Am closed its first sale, we were ready. We set out for the new hospital with our package—Pain/Train.

Training was scheduled in a large room just down the hall from the wing that would become the new Pain Treatment Center. When we assembled for the first morning's session, all of the new interdisciplinary staff members were present. Everything went well. Then, after the break, another person joined the group.

(At this point in the development of my change skills and knowledge, I had focused almost entirely on adopter stages and related strategies. What I had not yet learned much about was the importance of the organizational systems in which a change project is embedded.)

When we got to the first Q & A session, the new woman raised her hand. With an obvious sneer, she said, "I thought training was for dogs. Education is for people."

I responded, "You're certainly right. Education is for people. But, training is usually job-related when the performance wanted is well defined. That's true of most adult work-related instruction and that's why we called this 'training'."

The woman said nothing more though she continued to frown throughout the session. She left at the break and didn't return.

When we found out later that she was the hospital's Education Specialist and had learned about Pain/Train via rumors, we recognized our omission. Without even a courtesy call, let alone an invitation to participate, we had taken over her turf. We hadn't asked the systems question, "Is there anyone at the hospital other than the new staff who may be affected by the training?" While it was true that the woman couldn't stop us, she was likely to badmouth the program every chance she got. Not good! And that wasn't the last of our errors with regard to the system.

At lunchtime, I walked down the hall and stopped at the nurse's station for directions to the restroom. There were three nurses behind the counter and every one of them turned away from me. I asked again and finally one nurse turned and pointed the way to the restroom. No words, no smile. Again, I was surprised.

Later we learned that the hospital administration had decided to locate the new, profit-based pain program in the wing that these nurses' station served. This wing had for some time housed terminal patients, some of whom the nurses had become quite attached to. They were extremely upset to learn that their wing would be closed and their patients dispersed to nursing homes. Again, we had failed to ask the systems question—"Is there anyone in the hospital other than the new staff who may be affected by the pain program?"

So far, we had made two socially disruptive, but not ultimately lethal, mistakes. That one was still to come.

Within the year, Med-Am had contracts with two more hospitals and we continued to implement training. Then, one day I got a phone call from the President. The Company had been stopped from making sales to any more hospitals. How had this happened?

The Director of the VA Hospital in the state capital had contacted the Governor because they were losing their chronic pain patients to the new hospital programs and this was causing a loss of funds. The Governor issued a restraining order on Med-Am. Med-Am filed an appeal and, many months later, won its case. However, by then, their Board of Directors had decided it was imprudent to continue to fund this start-up company. Med-Am was out of business. Again, we had failed to ask the systems question—"Is there any organization or person external to the hospital who may be affected by this program?"

No one held me responsible for these failures. However, as I learned more about systems, I saw that, if I had taken the system into consideration and raised questions that the client might have followed up, the training and even the client company itself might have benefited.

The Med-Am case illustrates how important systems can be in a change project. Not only did the new pain program have an impact on the hospital and the people in it, but the people had an impact on the new pain program.

In the case of the hospital, there was a training delivery system already in place and we ignored it. Similarly, we ignored the social system of the ward we were displacing. As for the conflict with the VA system, that involved both the healthcare supplier system and the political system. All are examples of systems that could have been considered in advance.

In general, there is an expectation that a technical change will have an impact on the organization's technical systems and appropriate plans are made. However, change facilitators often fail to attend adequately to the impact a change may have on the people or other non-technical systems. Or, to the impact these systems may have on the change.

Your Change Project System

So what about your change project system? How can you identify all of the people and groups which are relevant to your particular project? The next graphic—another sociogram—illustrates one way you can get a clearer picture of your change project system.

Every person or group that may have an impact on the change or be impacted by it is represented. Of course, each change project's sociogram will be different and, in a real project such as yours, the names (or initials) of the people or groups would be included with their titles. Where needed, groups can be broken down into individuals, e.g., if major vendors relate in different ways, they should be shown individually.

By creating such a graphic of communication between significant people and groups, you can identify the strong and the weak points in the communication system and act accordingly. Then, you can take advantage of what's working and, hopefully, fix what isn't working.

Sample Sociogram of a Change Project System   The question addressed in this sociogram is—Insofar as the change project goes, who communicates (or should communicate) with whom and what is the status of that communication?

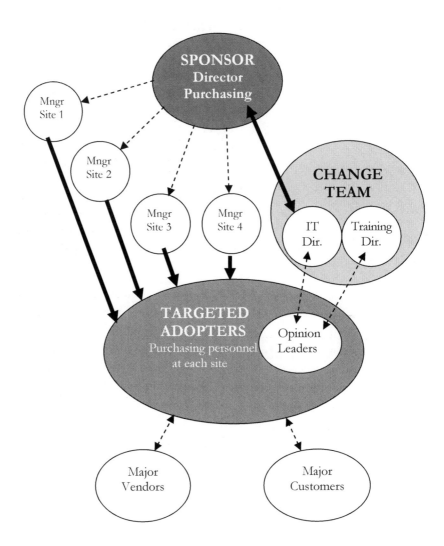

Arrows show the direction of communication.
Solid lines indicate good communication.
Dotted lines indicate poor communication.

The Purchasing Director is the SPONSOR. He has mandated the change and assigned the IT Director and the Training Director to make it happen. The solid 2-arrow line indicates that there is good, two-way communication between the Purchasing Director and the IT Director. However, the absence of a line indicates that there is no communication between the Purchasing Director and the Training Director. This means that the Training Director is dependent on the IT Director for information and guidance. If that's okay, fine. If not, something needs to be done to establish communication between the Director of Purchasing and the Training Director. (Especially if you're the Training Director.)

Also, the dotted lines between the Purchasing Director and the four site managers who are the BOSSES of the targeted ADOPTERS suggest that he hasn't communicated to them the importance of the change. Since they are in the authority line over the ADOPTERS and need to function as additional SPONSORS for the change, this can certainly cause a problem. Some action should be taken to encourage the Purchasing Director to use his influence and get the managers (BOSSES) aboard.

The managers (BOSSES) also need to communicate the change to both the vendors and the customers. The dotted lines suggest that, in this regard, communication is poor. Some action should be taken to improve the situation. Perhaps the most serious problem is that the CHANGE TEAM's communication with the OPINION LEADERS is weak. Fix it. Finally, in addition to outright communication gaps, there's also a lot of one-way communication in this organization—not the ideal for a change project.

Multiple Systems   In sum, a change project can be affected by many systems—the new one you create to manage the change and the existent ones that may affect or be affected by the change. The better you are able to recognize and align with all systems that may relate to your change, the less likely you are to be blindsided.

WORKSHEET 23   Make a sociogram for your entire change project system. Note especially poor communication links and what, if anything, you should do about them.

Project Balance Sheet

Another way to get a realistic look at your change project is to create a Project Balance Sheet (based on Lewin's force-field analysis). This involves identifying the forces that are working for the change and those that are working against the change. The goal is to be knowledgeable about the tug-of-war going on between these forces.

WORKSHEET 24 Create a Balance Sheet (It's even more valuable for Change Team members to do this and then compare and discuss the results.)

1. List Forces. On the left in the appropriate categories, list the forces that are positive for your change. On the right, list the forces that are against it.

2. Rate Forces. Once your lists are complete, go back and rate each force on the positive list according to the scales at the top left of the page. Write your ratings in the boxes to the left. Repeat for the negative list using the scales at the top right.

3. Sub-Total. When you have rated every item, sub-total positives and negatives in the boxes at the bottom.

4. Read Discussion Page.

Your Change Project Balance Sheet

FORCES FOR

5 decisively positive
4 very positive
3 positive
2 somewhat positive
1 only mildly positive

FORCES AGAINST

dangerously negative 5
very negative   4
negative   3
somewhat negative   2
only mildly negative 1

Positive Change Factors	Negative Change Factors

Positive Adopter Factors	Negative Adopter Factors

Positive Key Adopter Factors	Negative Key Adopter Factors

Positive Leadership Factors	Negative Leadership Factors

Positive Organizational Factors	Negative Organizational Factors

Positive Change Team Factors	Negative Change Team Factors

Positive Other Factors	Negative Other Factors

total

total

Discussion of Balance Sheet

CAUTION! This is not a precise measure. You could load one side with a lot of trivial forces which would result in a higher total for that side. Even with this weakness, the Balance Sheet can give you a rough idea of where your change project stands.

If It's Bad News It's obvious that if your sub-total for negatives is larger than your sub-total for positives, that's not good news. The greater the difference, the greater the jeopardy for your change project.

Can You Make It Good News?

- What are the one or two biggest forces going for your project? How can you maximize their positive effect?

- What are the one or two biggest forces against it? How can you minimize their effect?

- Are there other positive forces you can maximize? How? Other negative forces you can minimize? How?

Are There Make-or-Break Items? Another rating to consider is that of any make-or-break items. If the CEO of the organization has decided that the change will happen (e.g., Jack Welch, "Your business must be #1 or #2 in its market or it's gone."), regardless of how many negatives there are, this single positive is likely to dominate. Or in a manufacturing plant, if the union opposes the change, regardless of how many positives there are, this single negative may dominate. (In recent times, especially in the auto industry, this has not been the make-or-break item it once was.)

Do you have any make-or-break items? If so, consider them in your planning.

A Realistic Picture Whether the results are good or bad, you should now have a more realistic picture of your change project and that, in itself, is good. And, if there are problems, you may still be able to do something about them! (You may also want to revise your Action Plan to account for what you've learned here.)

13. Take Care of Yourself

A Change Agent's Survival Strategies

On top of lots of analysis and planning for all of the other people involved in a change project, change agents need to give some attention to their own survival. Why?

By now, you probably have some ideas about why, but here are a few reasons:

Multiple Skills Required You need a wide variety of skills, sometimes skills that seem almost in opposition, e.g., technical skills and people skills, management skills and leadership skills, goal-directed skills and participative skills.

Unpredictability Regardless of how well you plan ahead, the change process is filled with unpredictable events and frustrations.

Underestimated Role The change agent role is often underestimated and unappreciated even by those who ask you to fulfill it.

Invisibility The more successful you are, the more likely you won't be noticed or credited. Most of us like a bit of recognition for our efforts!

Demands The role involves lots of "giving" behaviors and not many "getting" responses. You listen, accept, understand, empathize, inform, respect and support. When do you get something?

Burn-out Job For all of these reasons, people involved in a series of change projects—whether as change agents or adopters—tend to burn-out. They need lots of R's—relaxation, refueling, recreation, restoration, reaffirmation, recognition, rejuvenation, renewal, and the biggest R of all—resiliency.

Daryl Conner says,

> *Resilient people face no less of a challenge than others when confronting a crisis, but they typically regain their equilibrium faster, maintain a higher level of quality and productivity in their work, preserve their physical and emotional health, and achieve more of their objectives than people who experience future shock.*

Some experts say that resiliency is the most important attribute change agents can have, at least for their own survival. Unfortunately, resiliency is like empathy in that you tend to have it or not to have it. If, because of your genetic make-up or your life experience, you just naturally have it, you'll always have an advantage. But, if you want to be more resilient, you can be—at least somewhat. Here are five strategies for being less stressed and more resilient. (Good for already resilient people too.)

1. Get someone to talk to. Two big reasons for having someone to talk to are (a) to get someone else's perspective and suggestions when you've run into a wall and (b) to be able to express your frustrations and anxieties without negative ramifications. This may or may not be the same person, but it almost always should be someone safely outside of the change project. Ask yourself—

> Who can you safely talk to *inside* the organization, but outside the change project and team?

> Who can you safely talk to *outside* the organization? Who will be an attentive and supportive listener?

2. Get what you need from your boss. If the change is to be successfully implemented, you and your team need the support of your bosses. Even if they are willing to provide support, they may require help to understand what you need. You need them to allocate *time* for work on the change project, not just add these new responsibilities onto regular tasks. You need them to provide *financial support* for project-related activities (e.g., meeting facilities, site visits, training development). You need them to make public and private *statements of support* for the change project. You need them to give *recognition and reward* for project successes.

In *Power and Influence*, John Kotter suggested these ways (adapted here) to get the support of bosses:

- ✓ Learn about the boss—needs, goals, pressures, strengths, weaknesses and working style.

- ✓ Learn about yourself—needs, goals, pressures, strengths, weaknesses and working style.

- ✓ Use the above information to develop a relationship that takes similarities and differences into consideration.

- ✓ Clarify mutual expectations, avoid ambiguity.

- ✓ Keep the boss informed. Surprises are not usually welcome.

- ✓ Be dependable and honest.

- ✓ Use the boss's time and resources carefully and selectively.

3. Don't take it personally. When your adopters and others complain and criticize the change, try not to take it personally. Remember that they're grieving at their loss of the way things were, they're anxious about the way things are, and they're concerned about the way things are going to be. It's probably about them, not you.

4. Be realistic about the project. Take your Balance Sheet seriously. Optimize positive forces, and beware of negatives! All change projects have positive forces, that's how they came to be. But, it's the negatives that can sink your project. If you have negatives, address them—the earlier the better. How? Share your concerns and the reasons for them with your team and with your sponsor. Obviously, you need to be diplomatic—not rushing in to say "Your pet project is in big trouble." Remember—people want to *kill the messenger* when the news is bad. But when the bad news is real and it's hidden, it tends to kill the change and sometimes even the change agent's job or the company itself.

One bit of advice—When at all possible, have a solution to offer when you point out a problem. For example, what's needed to make the change work? more time? additional resources? another sponsor? other people on the team? more user-involvement? what?

5. Take care of yourself. Up until the last few pages, the focus has been mostly on all of the other people involved in a change project. But change agents are people too, and they need to recognize the pressures likely to impinge on them. It helps to ask questions like these:

> In terms of your personal or professional growth, what is there for you to learn from this project?
>
> If the project fails, what plans do you have to take care of yourself?
>
> If the project succeeds, what will your sources of satisfaction be?

As you facilitate a change project, you may feel that it is you who is changing. In fact, if the project is a complex and long one, you almost certainly will be changed by the experience. It may be helpful to think of yourself—like your adopters—as going through a transition, one which may be personally somewhat turbulent.

The following Change Aid offers some suggestions for how to take care of yourself as you move through a transition. It may be useful for your adopters too.

Take Care of Yourself
(adapted from William Bridges' *Transitions*)

During transitions...

Take your time, don't act for the sake of action. Your insides may need to catch up with your outside. That is, your internal way of being and perceiving may take a while to catch up with your already changed external behaviors. There's stuff to be learned. Give yourself time.

Recognize why you're uncomfortable. It's natural for a transition to involve anxiety, threat to yourself and others around you, and pain. "Distress is not [necessarily] a sign that something is wrong but that something is changing."

Take care of yourself in little ways. "Find the little continuities when everything else seems to be changing." How might you take care of yourself in a small way?

Arrange temporary structures. If you're in a transition at work and you could use some help or indulgence, ask for it. You don't need it forever, and you can say so, but a little temporary support can tide you over. Be wise in your choice of a helper.

Use the transition as an opportunity to learn. "...what you are about to become will require new understandings and new skills you may not yet possess." Ask—What are these new demands likely to require of you? What new abilities or strengths might you find in yourself? What new skills might you try to learn?

WORKSHEET 25 Self-Assessment   Check the boxes that apply to you now. After you finish, read the discussion on the next page.

	DISAGREE	UNSURE	AGREE

The Change
- I understand the change fully.
- I personally believe in the change.
- The change is good for the organization.
- The change is good for the users.
- The change can be implemented.

The Users
- I am familiar with the users' knowledge of the change.
- I know how the users feel about the change.
- I understand the users' concerns regarding the change.
- I respect the discomfort/pain people feel when asked to change.
- I accept complaints and resistance as natural responses.

The Organization
- I know the organizational culture well.
- I know how the change relates to current strategy/initiatives.
- I know the sponsor(s) of the change well.
- I know the users' boss well.
- I know how to get resources for this change project.

My Credibility with Users
- Users see me as knowing the change.
- I am accepting of others' viewpoints and opinions.
- I am good at "reading" people.
- Users see me as having their interests in mind.
- Users trust me.

My Communication Skills
- I am a good stand-up communicator.
- I am a good interviewer.
- I am good at getting others to express their views.
- I am a good writer.
- I listen more than I talk.

My Meeting Skills
- In meetings, I actively participate and communicate my ideas.
- I do not dominate meetings.
- I am good at helping quiet people participate.
- I am good at not letting anyone dominate.
- I am good at defusing or refocusing conflicts.

My Survival Skills
- I use stress-reducing techniques myself.
- I am confident of my own value apart from this job & project.
- I accept that I alone cannot make this change happen.
- I have family or friends who are good sounding boards.
- I have mentors who give me good organizational advice.

Discussion of Your Self-Assessment

Q As you were responding, did you find yourself viewing any of the items differently from the way you did at the beginning?

Q When you compare the two assessments, did you rate some items quite differently? Look at any shifts and try to figure out why you changed? If you went down in an area, it may mean that now you're better informed and more realistic about what it takes to be an effective change agent.

Q Note that category labels (e.g., The Change, The Users) have been added. Do you have more than one weak item in a category? If so, this may be a clue regarding which areas you need to work on or fill with others' expertise.

If you've read this far, you already know the role is a challenging one, and I admit that not everyone welcomes challenges of this dimension. But I almost guarantee that, if you get through your change project alive, you will have grown in some important ways.

As it was in the Age of the Dinosaurs, those who can change are most likely to survive. If you can help your fellow men and women and yourself survive in this rapidly changing world—you are indeed doing something noble.

Q *Why would anyone want such a demanding and often precarious job as that of a change agent?*

A *Because it's challenging and maybe even noble.*

Communicate to Others "Where They Are"   Hopefully, as a result of what you've learned here, you will be more effective in your professional practice and in your personal life. But, remember, if you've bought into the ideas and actions proposed here, it's because you came through all the stages of adoption to get to this point. Be sure to communicate with others "where they are," and do what you can to make their changes palatable—like chocolate. Go with my best wishes!

If You Want to Read More

Many people have found *Transitions* by William Bridges to be useful in coping with life's changes, whether they are personal or organizational.

Invitation! As you apply the Chocolate Model in your own organizational work, you are likely to have experiences that can be of help to others. And others may have experiences that can be of help to you.

If we work together, we may be able to make your organizational changes more palatable. Share your successes, questions, stories, concerns, suggestions, etc. at

chocochange.com.

APPENDICES

Appendix A.   How to Select a Project

Think about an organizational change project you can work on throughout the book. It is best to pick a project that has the following characteristics.

✓ It's a real project for real people in a real organization.

✓ It's in the planning or pre-planning stage.

✓ Members of the group who are targeted to make the change are in communication with each other.

✓ They are available to you for observation and interviews.

✓ The group is of a size suitable for you to be able to identify all or at least the significant people in the group. (The Chocolate Model can be applied, in part or whole, to a group of any size but, since this will be your first application, it will work better if the group has approximately 7-25. If your group is quite large, you might select a sub-set.)

✓ You can be specific about the change, the adopters and the organization or the part of it in which the adopters work. The hardest part of this seems to be defining the change in specific terms. Can you describe in specific details what is it that you want people to buy into or do?

It may help to review in the following table some examples of change projects on which others have worked. (Note: These descriptions are abbreviated. For your project, be as specific and detailed as you can be.)

Organization	Change	Adopters
Corporate Supply Chain	Structured training program	13 intermarket supply planners
Agricultural conglomerate	"Cookbook" for improving implementation	12 project implementation leads
Technology corporation	New system to track higher level product deviations	9 Product Engineers, 5 Quality Control Techs, 3 Supervisors
Employment & Training Bureau at a State Dept. of Labor	Change from independent generalist to team specialist	26 consultants
Technology corporation department	Change from quality management system to just-in-time embedded system	16 project manager coaches
National department store chain	Performance-oriented problem solving	11 trainers & 3 managers
Church	New church childcare program	12 church leaders
Developmental disabilities agency	New reporting procedures	30 therapists
Technology corporation assembly department	New system to track higher level product deviations	9 Assembly Product Engineers, 5 Quality Control Technicians, and 3 Supervisors
Not-for-profit therapy horse agency	New grant-writing process	8-10 grant writers (director, consultant, 6-8 volunteers)
Military branch	Change from SME specialist instructor to cross-trained class mentor	12 chiefs/senior instructors

Appendix B. How to Make a Sociogram

1. List the names of the people in the group.

2. Imagine asking (or, better, actually ask) each person the question of your interest. For example, "Whose opinion would you most value regarding X [the change]?" "Whose opinion would you want in regard to X?" "Who has the best ideas with regard to X?" "Who has the most influence with regard to X?" etc. Write down the questions you asked.

3. Beside each name, write the name(s) of the person they chose (or, if you're just imagining this, the names of the persons you think they would choose).

4. When you've done everyone, go down the list and count how many times a person is chosen. Write that number by the person's name.

5. Now, begin your sociogram by putting the person or persons chosen the most near the center. Write their names in their circles.

6. Then place the others so that you have as few cross-overs as possible. This takes a bit of trial-and-error. For each person, draw an arrow to the person(s) s/he chose. (It may be wise to use a pencil so you can easily erase and move people around to avoid cross-overs as much as possible.)

7. Look for the names with the most arrows. These are the potential opinion leaders for your change.

8. Look for any cliques or isolates who may need special attention.

REMEMBER—If your sociogram is based on *your* opinions of how people would respond, it is just a reflection of your views. Hence, it may or may not be realistic. Consider any sociogram based on this kind of data as only a *possible* reflection of, or hypothesis about, the social relationships of the people. By far, the most reliable data comes from the people themselves.

Appendix C. An Interviewing Exercise

This exercise involves 4 parts to be done in order. Do **not** look ahead.

Interviewing Exercise—Part 1

Part 1 involves one interview of about 10 minutes length. You need a recorder.

The Recorder Before meeting with the interviewee, test the recorder with someone else to determine at what distance and in what position it will best pick up your two voices. It is important that, when you play the interview tape back, you can understand everything each of you said.

The Interviewee The interviewee can be a relative, friend, neighbor, or anyone not related to your change project.

Ahead of Time When you ask the person for an interview, say something like

> *A book I'm reading includes an exercise on interviewing. I'd appreciate it if you would let me interview you. It will only take about ten minutes.*

If they want to know what the interview is about, just say *"I have a couple of questions about technology."* If they say they don't know anything about technology, say *"That's all right. The questions are easy."* Do **not** mention the specific topic until you turn on the recorder and begin the interview.

The Topic of Your Interview For a topic, choose a technology such as a digital camera, cell phone, iPAD, Kindle, iPod, iPhone, Skype, Facebook, TiVo or some other similar innovation. However, be sure to pick a technology that meets the following requirements:

1. You have at least some experience with the technology.

2. The level of the technology generally matches the interviewee. That is, you might ask a teen-ager about the Facebook, whereas you might ask your grandmother about a digital camera. (Apologies to Grandmother, but you get the idea.)

3. You don't know the relationship between or history of the interviewee and the specific technology. In other words, this interview is real.

Your Interview Goal Your goal is to find out what the interviewee's history and current status is with the technology.

The Interview Begin by asking if they have or use the technology. (If they've never heard of it, ask about another technology.) Once you have a technology they've heard of, try to find out how they first heard of it, how they got information about it, whether they've had a demonstration or tried it out, and—if they're users—what finally moved them to adopt it.

How Long Should the Interview Be? Approximately 10 minutes. If you finish before that, just ask about another technology.

After you finish the interview, thank the interviewee, leave, and go to Part 2 which you do alone. Do not look ahead.

Interviewing Exercise—Part 2
This part involves transcribing, which is slow and tedious. It's also critical.

Transcribe your interview until you have 4 pages of transcript. Single space what one person says, but double space between different speakers. Indicate non-verbals in parentheses. Here's a sample:

> Norika: I'm hungry.
>
> John: Okay, where do you want to eat? We could go to The Siam House, or La Dolce Vita, or El Ranchero, or The Mikado, or we could just go to the MCI Cafeteria.
>
> Norika: Oh (sigh) I don't know.
>
> John: (laugh) That's what you always say.

For this to have value, you have to write exactly what people say. No editing, no enhancing, only what is said. Include every word, every sigh, laugh or groan, every sound or long pause. Also, indicate if both talk at once.

Suggested Procedure—Listen to a bit, type it up, rewind and re-listen to the same bit, make the necessary corrections and move on. Transcribing is a slow business, even when you have a transcription device, and you probably don't have one. Be prepared for it to take 3-4 times as long to transcribe a page of script as it does just to listen to the same taped dialogue.

The good news is that you're only transcribing the first 4 pages of each interview. Although people speak at different rates, that's likely to be less the full 10 minutes.

Go to Part 3.
Do not look ahead.

Interviewing Exercise—Part 3

Review these interviewing No-No's

Interrupting. For good communication, interrupting another speaker is a no-no. (Admittedly, there are people who would never stop talking if you didn't interrupt them.) Since the goal of most interviews is to get information from and about the interviewee, an interruption just breaks or stops the flow of information from the person.

Talking over. Talking at the same time as another speaker is not only rude and sends a message that you are not listening, but it increases the likelihood that you will miss what the interviewee is saying—the point of the interview.

Misleading inflection & unnecessary add-ons. Each language has a characteristic way of showing, through inflection, what the speaker's intent is. For example, an interviewer's tone sends a message that his/her question has come to an end. This is a signal for the interviewee to answer. However, some interviewers have the habit of seeming to end, then starting again—to restate the question in other words or expand on it. Unless the interviewee shows through word or facial expression the need for clarification, such add-on's only interrupt the interviewee's thought process.

Inserting yourself. Don't introduce details about who or what you know or feel about the topic. The goal is not to put your ideas forward; it's to find out what the interviewee knows, thinks, feels. If you think that sharing something about yourself will elicit more from the interviewee, one way to do this is to attribute it to someone else. For example, if an interviewee has sort of dried-up and you want to encourage him/her, you might think of saying, "I had a chance to try an iPhone out. I borrowed a friend's for an hour. That really helped me see what the iPhone was like." But, to do that inserts your life story into the conversation. An alternative way to achieve your original purpose is to attribute the message to some vague other, e.g., "Sometimes, people have a chance to try out someone else's iPhone and that helps them see what the iPhone is like."

Analyze your interview transcript

1. Re-read your transcript. Look for examples of No-No's. If you find any, indicate what kind it is—

> Interruption
> Talk-Over
> Misleading Inflection
> Unnecessary Add-on
> Inserting Self

2. Read the following transcript of an interviewer who wants information on why a man bought the car he did and what his level of satisfaction is.

A Sample Interview

Maria: *I heard that you got your car in 2005. How did you come to buy a hybrid car before they became popular?*

Paul: *Oh, I'd been reading about what the impact of pollution was on the planet, and I wanted to do my part.*

Maria: *So you bought because of the environment?*

Paul: *Well, I guess that was the main reason. Of course, I wanted to cut my gas consumption.*

Maria: *To save money?*

Paul: *Sure, everybody wants to save money, don't they!*

Maria: *I believe you got one of the first models. Were you concerned about whether they'd gotten all of the design kinks out?*

Paul: *Oh, I read everything I could lay my hands on about the technology and I got online and found a chat room with a few hybrid owners.*

Maria: *And they reassured you?*

Paul: *Pretty much. Ultimately, I just decided to go for it.*

Maria: *How has it worked out?*

Paul: *I'm fine with it.*

Maria: *What do your friends think?*

Paul: *I think most of them approve.* (He grinned..) *Even if they wouldn't buy one themselves.* (Sounding satisfied with himself.) *Not yet at least.*

Maria: *I get the feeling that you're kind of proud of owning a hybrid.*

Paul (grinning): *You're right. I am. From the beginning, it's made me feel good.*

Maria: *All in all, you seem quite satisfied with your purchase.*

Paul: *Yes, you could say that.*

It's clear from this script that Paul approves of hybrid cars, but what does Maria think about them? The answer is—*You don't know.*

No Opinion! Although Maria spoke as much as Paul did, at no time did she indicate how she felt about hybrid cars. That's one important indicator of a good interviewer.

No Judgment! While Maria may or may not approve of people who buy hybrids, you don't know what she thinks about them. Or about Paul. That's another indicator of a good interviewer.

And that's exactly the way it should be when you first set out to find out what your adopters think about the change. This is especially important in the *earliest stage* of your change project.

Don't sell the change!
Don't judge the adopter!

Before we further analyze Maria's interview of Paul, let's look at the goal and some techniques of active listening—the Yes-Yes's.

The Yes-Yes's. The goal of active listening is to understand where the other person is coming from. What is *their* view? What do *they* think or feel? What is *their* opinion? If you are the kind of person who is genuinely interested in other people—a big advantage for a change agent—you probably already use some of the following techniques.

SOME ACTIVE LISTENING TECHNIQUES

Neutral Questions If you want people to tell you what they think, avoid threatening questions. Ask neutral ones.

Follow-up Questions When you ask for more information, people usually give it. Amazing!

Reflections Reflecting (restating or paraphrasing) what the person said has two purposes. When you reflect what you think the person means by re-stating it in other words, you get a chance to find out if your understanding is correct. Also, when they hear their own message played back, they often elaborate and you get still more information.

Summations Summarizing from time to time or at the end can lead to clarification and also provide a sense of closure for both of you.

Now look at how Maria used these techniques in her simple interview of Paul.

Maria: *I heard that you got a hybrid car back in 2005. How did you come to buy a hybrid car before they became popular?* (NEUTRAL QUESTION)

Paul: *Oh, I'd been reading about what the impact of pollution was on the planet, and I wanted to do my small part.*

Maria: *So you bought because of the environment?* (REFLECTION)

Paul: *Well, I guess that was the main reason. Of course, I wanted to cut my gas consumption.*

Maria: *To save money?* (FOLLOW-UP QUESTION to check out an assumption of money, not just gas)

Paul: *Sure, everybody wants to save money, don't they!*

Maria: *I believe you got one of the first models. Were you concerned about whether they'd gotten all of the design kinks out?* (NEUTRAL QUESTION)

Paul: *Oh, I read everything I could lay my hands on about the technology and I got online and found a chat room with a few hybrid owners.*

Maria: *And they reassured you?* (FOLLOW-UP QUESTION)

Paul: *Pretty much. Ultimately, I just decided to go for it.*

Maria: How has it worked out? (NEUTRAL QUESTION)

Paul: *I'm fine with it.*

Maria: *What do your friends think?* (NEUTRAL QUESTION)

Paul: *I think most of them approve.* (He grinned.) *Even if they wouldn't buy one themselves.* (Sounding satisfied with himself.) *Not yet at least.*

Maria: I *get the feeling that you're kind of proud of owning a hybrid?* (based on his tone of voice, FOLLOW-UP QUESTION to explore other possible reasons)

Paul (grinning): *You're right. I am. From the beginning, it's made me feel good.*

Maria: *All in all, you seem totally satisfied with your purchase.* (SUMMATION)

Paul: *Yes, you could say that.*

Silence A technique not in the list above is silence. Yet it can be a powerful tool for getting additional information. While it's important not to cause the other person discomfort by too long a silence, sometimes, after a response, if you wait a bit, the other person will elaborate or add new information voluntarily. And sometimes that information is surprising and informative.

Nonverbal Messages Although nothing in the above transcript suggests that Maria was judging, the fact is she might have been giving non-verbal cues about her opinion of both hybrid cars and their owners. When you interview to learn your adopters' views, it's important not to let your non-verbals send unintended messages. But two non-verbal messages you *should* send are

✓ **INTEREST** *"I'm interested in what you're saying."*

✓ **RESPECT** *"I respect you, whatever your views are."*

Nonverbal means for expressing interest and respect include your

- eye contact
- tone of voice
- facial expressions
- body position

Go to Part 4.

Interviewing Exercise—Part 4

No more transcribing required!

Part 4 involves doing another (better?) interview.

1. Record another 10-minute interview with a different person. As before, select someone who is not related to your change project, and select a technology (a) that you are familiar with, (b) which is appropriate to the interviewee, and (c) about which you have no information regarding the interviewee's relationship or use.

Goal # 1: Same as before—to find out what the person's history and current status is with the technology.

Goal # 2: Even more important goal—to eliminate all No-No's and use as many Yes-Yes's as you can.

2. Listen to the tape. You might listen one time just to get a general idea of how it went. (And, yes, different interviewees can make a difference.) Then, listen again, especially looking to see if you've eliminated the No-No's and used some Yes-Yes's.

3. Make a note. So you won't forget, jot down what you learned about your strengths and weaknesses as an interviewer.

Return to Chapter 6.

Skim from page 72 to page 77 to be sure you didn't miss anything and also to note another Change Aid. Then begin to read again on page 78.

Appendix D. Interview Record Example

Randy Kirk is an Organizational Effectiveness Specialist at the Methodist Hospital in Houston, Texas. He interviewed three of his adopters (nurses) and noted their exact words. As time passes, he won't be dependent on memory which is often unreliable. Such a record will also make it easier to share valid data with his change team.

So you can read this in the context of Randy's change project, this is how he described it:

The Situation: Presently, different areas MAY use a checklist of a patient's needs, medications and other information necessary for pre/post op. Also individuals may use their own "homemade" checklist. So, instead of being asked once, the patient is routinely asked over and over the same questions, causing stress for the patient and the family members.

The Change: A single, consistent Checklist for Pre and Post Op use.

The Adopters: 35 Nurses in the Pre and Post Op areas

Adopters	Stage	Interview Notes – Qs & As
Nurses		*Questions Asked:* *"Whose opinion would you trust with regard to X?"* *"Who do you think would have the best ideas with regard to X?"* *"What two people would you ask if you wanted to know more about X?"* *Others for follow-Up on above questions and then "Is there anything else you'd like to tell me about your thoughts on this upcoming change?"*

| RA -
25 years as a
nurse | Curiosity

and

Mental Tryout

There were many personal concerns and opinions (as you can see)

And

She was looking at the job focus, how it would affect her workload and others in the immediate area. (Job Impact) | Some history of how this "New Checklist" has come into focus.

"It's supposed to make our work easier, less for us to do on this side"

"I trust myself and no one else" (she got confused about questions #1. She answered according to who she trusted to do the work ON the check-list and the patient, not about the change. But was still an interesting comment.)

"The Nurses in the group have the best ideas with regards to this change. I trust them all"

"I would go to the Manager or my charge nurse if I wanted to know more about this change"

"It's Horse Hockey!"

"The people on that side (Pre-Op) are allowed to do what they want and not held accountable"

"I know change is hard"

"If it works, it would be GREAT!" |
| GC – 28 years as a nurse | Curiosity with slight Awareness

GC had opinions, was well informed and looked at the process of the change from her work's point of view.

She also was on the slight "passive" side in the conversation as she did not think about the questions | "I trust the opinion of the area nurses (Post Op) and the manager input in this change. We deal with the patient every day and this is why we are here. To help the patient. This is what this change will do – help the patient."

"The best ideas about this check-list would come from the Unit Secretary and the Nurses of this unit (Post Op)."

"The two people I would ask for more information are the Manager and the Charge Nurse. The Charge nurse is a member of this Change Committee and |

	too long. She answered straight-forward and to the point. This is not a fair statement, but you just had to be there.	so that is the logical place to go for more information."
		"This will be an improvement."
		"It will help us manage our work."
		"This will help us facilitate patient care"
NE – 6 Years as a nurse	Mental Tryout And Hands-On Tryout NE has thought through how the change will work and seeking information from Co-workers that do "Research" and seeks information from department leadership. Could this be a generational difference?	"I trust the opinion of the Director and the Manager. They are open to change and trying things out as pilots. They have the knowledge base and experience from both a staff and a leadership point of view." "The best ideas for the check-list will come from Liz. She has worked both Pre and Post Op and can see it from both sides." "The 2 people I would get information from is Norma in Pre-Op because she does "Research" and can tell you about things and makes it exciting! And Chris in Post Op because she is so artistic, she can help you visualize what she wants you to see. That helps me." "I like it…I am open to change and things can only get better. I get excited by new challenges and new ideas." "I think it will work if everyone understands the concepts and know how efficient it will make our work."

He also analyzed their quotes according to CBAM's stages of concerns.

Possible Resistance Reasons	Possible Acceptance Reasons
SELF	**SELF**
"Another Change!"	"It's done FOR me, it's easy !"
"I did not get a Say-So in this new form"	"All I have to do is refer to it or review it!"
"The group that is working on this does not know my job as well as I do"	"It makes my work easier"
TASK	**TASK**
"Another form to deal with"	" My Department leadership made it mandatory"
OTHER	**OTHER**
"We've tried this before and it did not work"	" The co-workers I trust thought it was a good idea....so I thought it was too"
"This can't be in the Medical Records so we can't use it !" " I don't use the on-line system during this part of my work so it's no use to me"	

After doing these interviews, he said, *"I found the interviews to be VERY interesting and can't wait to do this again on another project."*

Appendix E: Action Plan Examples

Since every change project is different, the details of each action plan are also different. Even so, it may help to see examples of others' action plans. Two are offered here. The first involves a significant change in the roles of some Coast Guard instructors. The second involves the change to a new software system for processing money movements in a brokerage call center.

Action Plan No. 1 by Marcus Gherardi

The CHANGE: Instructor role will change from subject-matter specialist to cross-trained instructor & class mentor

The ADOPTERS: 12 chiefs/senior instructors

The ORGANIZATION: US Coast Guard Maritime Law Enforcement Academy

STAGE & STRATEGY	MESSAGE	ACTIONS	PEOPLE	DATES	RESOURCES	LEADERSHIP
IF Awareness THEN Advertise	"This is where we are and this is where we need to be" – based on honest facts. We're going to do this as a team. We're going to enhance our leadership, professionalism, and future marketability.	Conduct all-hands meeting to inform staff of impending change.	Commanding Officer Executive Officer Training Officer Command Master Chief MLEA Staff	Week 1	Auditorium 30 minutes first thing in morning Examples of why the change is needed (ie: MISHAPS in the field from current program, video testimonials of unmet performance expectations in the field, etc)	All Sponsors (FC-5/FC-51) Opinion Leaders, Change Agents (MLEA): Demonstrate commitment from senior leadership by being on-hand at meeting with MLEA staff. Present a clear and unified message from FC-5, FC-51 and the MLEA that illustrates a desirable, future state of the MLEA following the proposed change.

STAGE & STRATEGY	MESSAGE	ACTIONS	PEOPLE	DATES	RESOURCES	LEADERSHIP
IF Curiosity THEN Dialogue	"The MLEA understands your individual concerns and have answers and a solid strategy in place to help mitigate your fears" "We are prepared to answer your questions."	Establish intranet website on change. Include a FAQ and a blog area where supervisors can address issues and concerns. Supervisors to schedule one-on-one meetings or conduct roundtable discussions on change (use LEAPS – see 'resources')	Commanding Officer Executive Officer Training Officer Command Master Chief MLEA Staff	Weeks 1 -3	Use LEAPS: *Listen* *Empathize* *Ask Questions* *Paraphrase* *Summarize* Develop "fact-sheet" to present "ah-ha" solutions to the most common anticipated questions. Have supervisors allocate 15 min for each individual.	FC-5/FC-51: Encourage questions from MLEA staff. Design/Develop and implement web-based video messages to communicate benefits of change. MLEA (Opinion Leaders and Change Agents): Brief adopters on rewards & incentives in place.
IF Mental Tryout THEN Demonstrate	"Our organization is ready for this change." "This change will be good for my future."	Video examples of where a similar change works. (ie: conduct video taped interviews with Company Commanders, Training Officer, and CO of USCG Basic Training). Highlight their success and build mental models where change will be successful at MLEA.	Opinion Leaders at USCG Basic Training Center, Cape May, NJ. MLEA Staff	Weeks 3 - 6	Schedule interviews at USCG TRACEN Cape May, NJ Allocate 3 days for interviews and 3 days for editing content.	FC-5/FC-51: Mitigate resistance to change by communicating directly with those staff members who are expressing concerns. Begin publicizing MLEA staff efforts. MLEA: Consolidate common adopter concerns and address publically ASAP. Demonstrate commitment to change by sacrificing personal schedule to meet adopter needs. (redistributing collateral duties, providing additional mentoring, etc.)

STAGE & STRATEGY	MESSAGE	ACTIONS	PEOPLE	DATES	RESOURCES	LEADERSHIP
IF Hands-on Tryout THEN Train	"The MLEA has a well-thought-out strategic plan in place to help everyone manage this transition."	Analyze, Design, Develop, and Implement action plan to effectively facilitate change for adopters: Job Task Analysis of the new position. Gap Analysis of knowledge & skill gap. Develop training schedule.	Training Officer MLEA Staff MLEA Team A (Program Pilot Team)	Weeks 1- 32 *NOTE:* Initial analysis would be conducted prior to the awareness stage. Design, development, and implementation would involve adopter feedback.	Time: 8 Weeks 2 weeks= final preps 6 weeks = pilot course Pilot Team Development Training Syllabus Trainer Schedule Debriefing schedule & data collection	FC-5/FC-51: Conduct personal phone calls to late adopters (communicate encouragement by demonstrating unyielding sponsor commitment) Spend increased time at MLEA (rather than HQ) Publicize MLEA success stories. MLEA: Publicly praise involvement/course improvement suggestions by pilot team or other adopters. Implement increased morale activities. Highlight adopter's positive change efforts on employee reviews.
IF Adoption THEN Support	"The Command is walking the talk." "MLEA has not strayed from original message in the awareness and curiosity stage."	- Conduct evaluations on pilot program and modify as appropriate. - Ensure effective information network of keeping staff informed. - Ensure best tools are available for staff to do their new job. - Ensure worthy incentives are in place to reward staff for sacrifices.	Commanding Officer Executive Officer Training Officer Command Master Chief	Weeks 32 and beyond	3-4 weeks for program evaluation.	FC-5/FC-51: Provide resources for program sustainability. Seek FORCECOM support for additional public recognition (Flag visits – presentation of meritorious unit commendation, etc) MLEA: Remove final barriers to change (laggards, logistical constraints) Ensure that rewards/incentives that were promised in the awareness stage are provided. Set new program goals and continue to encourage adopter feedback.

Action Plan No. 2 by Tiffini Sorcic

The CHANGE: new SmartStation system to process money movements
The ADOPTERS: 7 Service & Trading representatives (later 150)
The ORGANIZATION: Brokerage Call Center

STAGE & STRATEGY	MESSAGE	ACTIONS	PEOPLE	DATES	RESOURCES	LEADERSHIP
IF Awareness THEN Advertise	Pre-emptive message during the "Change Management" manager-led explaining how and why systems and processes are being selected for go-forward integration (putting us on the path of where we want to be). Brief announcement of how funds transfer requests will be processed at integration.	Develop talking points about system and processes selection for integration to be delivered during Change Management sessions. Have a respected member of the management team (Call Center Director) send an email announcement to the representatives.	Call Center manager (Kathy) to deliver pre-emptive message during Change Management sessions. Tiffini – write email announcement for Kathy to send (Kathy to modify if desired). Kathy to send brief email announcement to all Service and Trading representatives.	Pre-emptive message – happening this week (based upon questions I received in an early integration training class). Brief announcement to be sent mid- October.	Pre-emptive message was delivered during an existing training, not much req'd for resources. Brief announcement will only take about 30 minutes to draft.	Tiffini to draft brief announcement about the upcoming change. Amy to review drafted announcement, make any changes, if desired. Kathy to look over draft, edit if desired, and send to the floor.

STAGE & STRATEGY	MESSAGE	ACTIONS	PEOPLE	DATES	RESOURCES	LEADERSHIP
IF Curiosity THEN Dialogue	Frequently asked questions (with answers) based upon adoptee questions and concerns	Conduct more interviews with many different segments of reps to see what questions and concerns they have with this change. Compile a FAQ document that supervisors can cover in their weekly staff meetings. Ask supervisors to create a list of any question that comes up that may not be on the FAQ doc, and I will provide a follow up document with the answers. Post FAQs and updated FAQs to the Funds Transfer intranet page.	Tiffini – conduct interviews Adopters from several segments for interviewing. Tiffini – compile FAQ document. Amy (SME) – review FAQ document for accuracy. Supervisors – review FAQ doc in staff meetings, answer questions, note any questions that they cannot answer and give to me. Tiffini – update FAQ doc after staff meetings. Communications team – post FAQ doc. to Intranet.	Interviews are ongoing while materials are being developed. FAQ prepared and delivered in late October.	Interviews will take some time, especially to uncover rep's questions and concerns and find themes for the FAQ – 16 hours FAQ preparation – 4 hours FAQ sessions occurring during existing meetings FAQ updates – 2 hours	Sponsor (Amy) to speak with supervisory team about covering FAQs in team meeting. Sponsor (Amy) to review FAQ doc; provide input. Opinion Leaders to provide input to FAQ doc. to ensure questions are valid and let Tiffini know if other questions or concerns are being voiced on the floor. Communications (Steph) to post updated FAQ document to Intranet.

A-STAGE	MESSAGE	ACTIONS	PEOPLE	DATES	RESOURCES	LEADERSHIP
IF Mental Tryout THEN Demonstrate	Simplicity and similarities (to current process) of processing funds transfer requests using SmartStation	• Work with respected Opinion Leaders to show a demonstration of how quick and easy funds transfer requests are to process in SmartStation. • Prepare a document beforehand that describes the similarities and differences of the current and new systems for a hand out.	• T – ensure Opinion Leaders are comfortable providing a demonstration. • A.S., F.B., and possibly K.A. to conduct demonstrations. • T – prepare similarities and differences handout.	Demonstration to occur middle of November	• Prep and delivery time will be about 24 hours	T and AA (sponsor) to work with Opinion Leaders of what functionality to demonstrate and answers to difficult questions that may arise. Opinion Leaders to prepare for demonstration. Amy (sponsor) to review document about similarities and differences.

A-STAGE	MESSAGE	ACTIONS	PEOPLE	DATES	RESOURCES	LEADERSHIP
IF Hands-on Tryout THEN Train	• Pertinent details for adopters to use SmartStation for funds transfers requests. • Support structure that will be in place for implementation • Rewards and recognition plan.	• Classroom, hands-on training, so adopters can gain experience and confidence processing funds transfer requests using SmartStation. • Job aids for reference when the change is implemented. Information about post-implementation support will be listed on the job aid. • Create a motivating and energizing handout and posters announcing the rewards and recognition programs/events that are being rolled out with the integration.	T– Design, develop, and deliver SmartStation training, including job aids and rewards and recognition handout. • AA (proj SME) to review all training. • A.S., E.B, and K.A. (maybe) – to facilitate some classes. T, A.S. and E.B. – create posters for rewards and recognition.	Design and development must be done by November 5th. Recognition handouts and posters must be done before training takes place. Training to take place the 2nd week of December	• Approx. 80 developme nt hours (and a lot of effort). • About 60 hours in the classroom to train all 150 reps.	O (technical PM) and AA (sponsor) to provide Ti with any pertinent details for training. Olivia, Amy, A.S., and E.B. to review materials and provide feedback. A.S. and E.B. learn materials for training and assist in delivering the training. Tiffini, A.S. and E.B. – create posters for rewards and recognition.

A-STAGE	MESSAGE	ACTIONS	PEOPLE	DATES	RESOURCES	LEADERSHIP
IF Adoption THEN Support	Recognition for successful adoption. Support is available. "The Command is walking the talk." "MLEA has not strayed from original message in the awareness and curiosity stage."	Create weekly and daily email announcements letting reps know when lunches or dinners will be brought in and when the refreshment carts will be around. Ensure that the management team is sending appreciation emails to the reps thanking them for their hard work and efforts. Ensure that we have enough resources "walking the floor" and in the Command Center, so reps have support for this application change (and all of the others). Conduct evaluations on pilot program and modify as appropriate. Ensure effective information network of keeping staff informed. Ensure best tools are available for staff to do their new job. Ensure worthy incentives are in place to reward staff for sacrifices	Communications team – develop and deliver weekly and daily announcements. C (L&D Mgr) – follow up with peers to ensure thank you emails being sent. Commanding Officer Executive Officer Training Officer Command Master Chief	Begins MLK 2011 weekend will continue for approximately 2-3 weeks – possibly longer depending on call volumes (more volumes, the longer it will last). Weeks 32 and beyond	I am not privy to the budget or how much is being spent (and how frequently) with the integration; I am quite sure it will be several thousand dollars. There will also be a time and effort factor since the management team delivers the snacks via the snack cart to the reps.	T, AA, A.S. and E.B. – floor walking or command center duty. S to send communications to the floor (weekly and daily announcements) All management team – refreshment duty and thank you emails (presumably drafted by project team and sent on behalf of). Overall integration committee is responsible for planning the rewards and recognition for the conversion.FC-5/FC-51: Provide resources for program sustainability. Seek FORCECOM support for additional public recognition (Flag visits – presentation of meritorious unit commendation, etc) MLEA: Remove final barriers to change (laggards, logistical constraints) Ensure that rewards/incentives that were promised in the awareness stage are provided. Set new program goals and continue to encourage adopter feedback.

END NOTES

Chapter 1 Introduction

2. The Burning Platform There are many different versions of this story. The most likely basis for the business version is the 1988 disaster at the Piper Alpha oil production platform operated by Occidental Petroleum in the North Sea. According to Wikipedia, the death toll was 167 with 59 surviving. Other stories report different numbers.

4. Greensburg, Kansas Late on May 4, 2007, Greensburg was hit by a tornado that leveled 95 percent of the city and killed twelve people. Afterward, the city council voted to rebuild Greensburg at a LEEDS platinum standard. It is the first US city to become a "green" town.

6. Hybrid Corn Seed According to Everett Rogers who wrote the classic *Diffusion of Innovation*, this is "the most influential diffusion study of all time." (pp. 31-35)

8. Sailors Resist a Change This story came from Brett Christensen, Canadian Forces, Canadian Defence Academy, Directorate of Learning Innovation.

10. CACAO Some years ago, I decided that, as a change agent—if you understood and planned for four dimensions of the change project—you would be in pretty good shape. My first effort to communicate this was as the ABCD Model (Adopters, Blackbox, Change, Domain) in several publications. But I was never entirely satisfied with the acronym or with the order of presentation. When I finally decided that the best order for teaching the model was Change, Adopters, Change Agent, and Organization, I was surprised to find that the acronym was CACAO. Since cacao is the source of chocolate, the logical next step was the Chocolate Model.

Chapter 2 The Change

16. Change Characteristics With the exception of "social impact" which I have added, the change characteristics of the Chocolate Model are based on those proposed by Everett Rogers in Chapter 5 of *Diffusion of Innovations*, "Attributes of Innovations and Their Rate of Adoption." (2003, The Free Press)

17. Dinner's On! The story about insects as a food source is from Bryan Walsh's article, "Eating Bugs." It appeared in *Time Magazine*, May 29, 2008.

18. Tom Offers Charlie a Change This Tom Friedman interview took place on the PBS *Charlie Rose Show*, August 16, 2007.

Chapter 3 Why People Resist

28. Mager, Bob After four decades and many awards, Robert F. Mager is still the most widely read writer in training and education. His eight easy-to-read books (which include *Analyzing Performance Problems: Or You Really Oughta Wanna—How to*

Figure Out Why People Aren't Doing What They Should Be, and What to Do About It co-authored with Peter Pipe) have sold over 3,000,000 copies worldwide. His approach is the basis for many university courses in instructional design. One of his lesser known works—*The How to Write a Book Book*—is a helpful and encouraging guide for the aspiring writer. It encouraged me.

29. Five Stages of Grief Elizabeth Kubler-Ross proposed the five stages of grief in *On Death and Dying*. (1969, Macmillan; 1997, Scribner's) Wikipedia says, "The work of George Bonanno has shown that the stages model of grief has no scientific basis. A 2000–2003 study of bereaved individuals conducted by Yale University obtained some findings that were consistent with the five-stage theory and others that were inconsistent with it. Several letters were also published in the same journal criticizing this research and arguing against the stage idea."

30. I Just Want to Get Out of Here—Or Do I? This story is from Dana Jennings' article, "Losing a Comforting Ritual Treatment,." It appeared in the *New York Times*, June 30, 2009.

31. Kurt Lewin (1890-1947) Social psychologist Lewin is often called the father of social psychology. He was also a pioneer in organizational and applied psychology. Among his contributions are this change model and force-field analysis which is the basis for the Chocolate Model's Project Balance Sheet offered in Chapter 12 "The Big Picture."

31. *"I found Lewin's basic change model..."* This quote is from an article by Edgar Schein, "Kurt Lewin's Change Theory in the Field and in the Classroom: Notes Toward a Model of Managed Learning," *Systems Practice*, 1996. Schein is known for his work in organizational development. His books include *Process Consultation*, which I recommend if you are a consultant.

32. "our emotional side is an Elephant..." This quote is from *Switch: How to Change Things When Change is Hard* by Chip and Dan Heath. (2010, Broadway Books) They offer an interesting analogy (which they credit to Jonathan Haidt's *The Happiness Hypothesis*) for guiding your change efforts. They suggest that people have both a Rider (rationality) and an Elephant (emotion) which compete with each other, but are both necessary if change is to be made. They also propose that attention must be given to the Path you want people to use as they move toward the change. They include many good stories which may give you ideas for your own project.

33. Gloves! Gloves! Gloves! This story is from *The Heart of Change* by John P. Kotter and Dan S. Cohen (2002, Harvard Business School Press. pp. 29-30). They offer Kotter's 8-step guide to bringing about change (from Kotter's earlier *Leading Change*), as well as great examples which can stimulate you to think about your own activities in new ways. The "glove" example is the most creative tactic I've ever heard and it appeals to both the cognitive (My Gosh! Look how much we're paying for our gloves!) and the emotional (How embarrassing!).

37. BOHICA   Eric Abrahamson, Columbia U. Business School professor, introduced   BOHICA in "Change Without Pain," *Harvard Business Review*, July-August, 2000.

39. Another Reason to Resist—Health The original stress test was developed by two medical doctors, Thomas H. Holmes & Richard H. Rahe. It first appeared in "The Social Readjustment Rating Scale," *Journal of Psychosomatic Research*, 11(2), August 1967, pp. 213-218.

41. CBAM The Concerns-Based Adoption Model (CBAM) was developed in the 60s by Francis Fuller, a University of Texas professor. Later, a research group at U. of T. developed the model further. In the late 70s, one researcher, Gene Hall, introduced me to CBAM and also to the idea that systematic analysis and planning could facilitate a change. My eyes were opened! *Implementing Change: Patterns, Principles, and Potholes* (2010, 3rd ed., Prentice Hall), by Gene Hall and Shirley Hord describes CBAM in detail.

41. *"When a broad and significant change…"* This quote is from *Discontinuous Change* by David A. Nadler, M.S. Gerstein, R. B. Shaw & Associates. (1995, Jossey-Bass p. 602)

42. *"I don't get it…"* This quote is from Rick Maurer, author of *Beyond The Wall of Resistance.* (1996, Bard Press)

Chapter 4 Adopters

46. Adopter Stages Various researchers have proposed different adopter stages. In *Diffusion of Innovations* (Chapter 5, "The Innovation-Diffusion Process"), Everett Rogers describes five stages: knowledge, persuasion, decision, implementation, and confirmation. The University of Texas group that developed the Concerns-Based Adoption Model (CBAM) describe seven stages: awareness, information, personal, management, consequence, collaboration, and refocusing. In *Strategies for Planned Change*, Zaltman and Duncan describe eight stages: perception, motivation, attitude, legitimation, trial, evaluation, adoption/rejection, and resolution. In *The Heart of Change*, Kotter and Cohen describe three stages: see, feel and change. Lewin describes three stages—unfreeze, transition, and refreeze. An analysis of these models, as well as others not given here, will show that while the details and labels are different, they have much in common.

The five stages of the Chocolate Model—awareness, curiosity, mental tryout, hands-on tryout, and adoption—reflect the commonalities of the earlier research-based models. However, they have been designed with the goal of simplicity and easy application by organizational practitioners.

Lewin's three-stage model, described in some detail in Chapter 2, maps well onto the Chocolate Model. His "unfreeze" stage is roughly equivalent to the Chocolate Model's "awareness" stage; his "transition" stage is roughly equivalent to the middle three stages of the Chocolate Model, and his "refreeze" stage is roughly equivalent to the Chocolate Model's "adoption" stage.

48. Tony Marker Anthony W. Marker is Associate Professor in Boise State University's Department of Instructional & Performance Technology.

50. Trektel's New Purchasing Processes This example is from a consultancy of mine. Names have been changed.

Chapter 5 Adopter Group

57. "Opinion leaders..." The quote is from *The Change Agent's Guide to Innovation in Education* by Ronald G. Havelock. (1973, Educational Technology Publications, p. 120)

59. "A social system is a set..." The quote is from *Diffusion of Innovation* by Everett M. Rogers. (2003, The Free Press, p. 37)

59. Facebook An electronic social network launched in 2004 and, as of 2011, involving 600,000,000 of the world's people.

59. A Tool for Understanding This tool, the sociogram, was developed by Jacob L. Moreno (1889-1974) who taught at Columbia and New School for Social Research. A psychiatrist, he became interested in groups and pioneered group psychotherapy. Sociograms picture patterns of group interaction. They can be based on various criteria, e.g., social relations, lines of communication, channels of influence. Software for drawing sociograms is available online—some free, some commercial.

62. "Only 12 of the group members..." This quote is from Marshal B. Anderson's article "Interaction and Group-making in Online Learning Communities." It is available at http://www.marshal.co.uk/telematics/articles/ws2co_op/results.htm

64. Adoption Curves Rate-of adoption is commonly shown in a bell curve (dark line below) which is not cumulative. That is, each point on the curve represents the number of adopters adopting *at that point* in time. The S-curve (gray line below) is an alternative way of showing the same data. The S-curve is cumulative and each point on the curve represents the total number of adopters who have adopted *up to that point* in time.

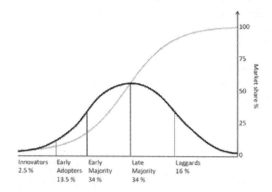

64. Footnote In *Diffusion of Innovation*, Everett M. Rogers says, "'Laggard' might sound like a bad name. This title of the adopter category carries an invidious distinction (in much the came way that 'lower class' is a negative nomenclature)...Diffusion scholars who use adopter categories in their research do not mean any particular disrespect by the term 'laggard.' Indeed, if they used any other term instead of laggards, such as 'late adopters,' it would soon have a similar negative connotation. But it is a mistake to imply that laggards are somehow at fault for being relatively late to adopt. System-blame may more accurately describe the reality of the laggards' situation. (2003, The Free Press, p. 285)

65. "The salient value of the innovator..." The quote is from *Diffusion of Innovation* by Everett M. Rogers. (2003, The Free Press, p. 283)

65. "The point of reference for the ... [traditionalist]..." The quote is from *Diffusion of Innovation* by Everett M. Rogers. (2003, The Free Press, p. 284)

68. Something Else to Think About Two recent, best-selling books have a close kinship to Rogers' adoption curve.

One is Malcolm Gladwell's *The Tipping Point* (2002, Little Brown & Company). If you've read it, you know that it's fun to read, it's based on research, and it has practical advice for change agents. What is the tipping point? In short, it's the point where the acceptance of an idea or product or message becomes an epidemic. Gladwell suggests that, with anything new, it is those few people on the front end (e.g., the innovators and early adopters) who determine the fate of the change. If you can get them, your change will become contagious and—as with a virus—the rest will rapidly follow.

The other book that relates to Roger's curve is Geoffrey Moore's *Crossing the Chasm* (2002, Collins Business Essentials). Moore is a marketing consultant whose emphasis is on high technology. He proposes that, while there is a gap between each of the categories of Rogers' curve, that gap becomes a chasm when it is between the early adopters and the early majority and that—insofar as the change goes— those to the left of the chasm are radically different from those to the right.

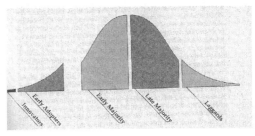

According to Moore, those to the left (innovators and early adopters) will buy a new technology even though it's expensive and clunky to use, but the majority won't buy until the price comes down and it's easy to use. One example is the desktop computer. In its earliest days, the first desktop computers were owned only by geeks willing to lay out significant cash, as well as to do the assembly and cope with the device's limitations. Only when the kinks were out (well, mostly out) and the cost was much less did the majority buy one.

Chapter 6 Data Gathering

73. Footnote Philip Kotler, Distinguished Professor of International Marketing at the Kellogg School of Management at Northwestern University, is the nation's best-known and most respected professional and author in the field of marketing. His *Marketing Management* is the world's most widely used textbook in marketing. His *Principles of Marketing* is in its 12th edition and continues to get rave reviews.

Robert Miller, with colleagues, is the author of *Strategic Selling* (1888) and *The New Strategic Selling* (2005). Both men propose ethical, win-win approaches to their professions.

78. For Fun—Watch Charlie Rose On PBS five nights a week, Rose interviews a myriad of famous people. While the interviews are usually informative and interesting and the show has maintained its popularity, Rose breaks many of the rules of good interviewing. Recent shows are available free online at The Charlie Rose Show; archival shows are for sale.

Chapter 7 Change Agent Strategies

81. Change Agent Strategies Influenced by Rogers and others, Chocolate Model strategies and related tactical actions are prescriptive and designed for immediate use by organizational practitioners.

88. Ken Kovach's Rewards Study Ken Kovach's study on rewards, "Employee Motivation: Addressing a Crucial Factor in Your Organization's Performance," appeared in *Human Resource Development (1999)* and is available online. http://www.accessmylibrary.com/article-1G1-17406645/employee-motivation-addressing-crucial.html

90. *Get Weird!* As suggested, this book is worth having on your shelf when you're looking for ideas. *Get Weird! 101 Innovative Ways to Make Your Company a Great Place to Work* by John Putzier (2001, American Management Association).

90. Rosabeth Moss Kanter In *1001 Ways to Reward Employees* (p. 4), Bob Nelson gives Kanter's seven guidelines for recognizing employees. Here they are in somewhat abbreviated form:

Principle 1: Emphasize success rather than failure.
Principle 2: Deliver recognition and reward in an open and publicized way.
Principle 3: Deliver recognition in a personal and honest manner.
Principle 4: Tailor your recognition and reward to the unique needs of the people involved.
Principle 5: Timing is crucial. Recognize contribution throughout a project. Reward contribution close to the time an achievement is realized. Time delays weaken the impact of most rewards.
Principle 6: Strive for a clear, unambiguous, and well-communicated connection between accomplishments and rewards.
Principle 7: Recognize recognition. That is, recognize people who recognize others for doing what is best for the company.

90. *1001 Ways to Reward Employees* By Bob Nelson, this book (2005, Workman) is not only full of good, often low-cost, ideas, it also offers organizing principles for when to do what and why.

96. If You Want to Read More   Nancy Torkewitz, a soft skills trainer for 4000+ employees at Syngenta, a global agri-products company. gives a testimonial for *The Heart of Change* by John Kotter and Dan Cohen (2002, Harvard Business School Press, p. 12).

Chapter 8 More Tactics—New and Old

99. E-mail Wikipedia says "The history of modern, global Internet email services reaches back to the early ARPANET. Standards for encoding email messages were proposed as early as 1973). Conversion from ARPANET to the Internet in the early 1980s produced the core of the current services. An email sent in the early 1970s looks quite similar to one sent on the Internet today.

99. How to Write an Email That Inspires...   This directive on how to write an email is from *The Dragonfly Effect: Quick, Effective, and Powerful Ways to Use Social Media to Drive Social Change* by Jennifer Aaker and Andy Smith (2010, Jossey-Bass. p. 6).

100. The case of the young entrepreneur (Sameer Bhatia) ...   This story of the young man who needed a bone-marrow transplant has appeared in several places. I first read about it in "Small Change" by Malcolm Gladwell (*The New Yorker*, October 4, 2010). The report here is based on the version told by Jennifer Aaker and Andy Smith in *The Dragonfly Effect* (2010, Jossey-Bass, pp. 1-17).

100. *"Dear Friends..."* This quote is from Robert Chatwani's e-mail quoted in *The Dragonfly Effect* by Jennifer Aaker and Andy Smith (2010, Jossey-Bass, p. 5).

103. Facebook The social network service, Facebook, was launched in February 2004. As of January 2011, it has more than 600 million users. The name Facebook is from the university publications aimed at helping students get to know each other.

103. *"A social system..."* The quote is from *Diffusion of Innovation* by Everett M. Rogers.(2003, The Free Press, p. 37).

104. If You Want to Read More   The book noted, *The Dragonfly Effect: Quick, Effective, and Powerful Ways to Use Social Media to Drive Social Change*, is by Jennifer Aaker and Andy Smith (2010, Jossey-Bass). Two other books that recommend social networking as a way to bring about social change are *The Networked Nonprofit: Connecting with Social Media to Drive Change* by Beth Kanter and Allison H. Fine (2010, Jossey-Bass) and *Share This! How You Will Change the World with Social Networking* by Deanna Zandt (2010, Berrett-Koehler),

105. *"Tell me the facts and I'll learn..."* According to Wikipedia, this is an Indian proverb.

105. John Kotter   Kotter is a management professor at the Harvard School of Business. He has written a number of best selling business books, e.g., *Power and Influence* (1985), *Leading Change* (1996), *A Force for Change* (1990), *The Heart of Change* (2002). All are worth your time.

105. Malcolm Gladwell   Gladwell is a staff writer for *The New Yorker*. He has written several best-selling books—*Blink, The Tipping Point, Outliers, What the Dog Saw: And Other Adventures*—and many articles. He selects an area to research and comes up with interesting and explanatory insights related to the area. In "Small Change" (*The New Yorker*, October 4, 2010), he critiques social networks such as Facebook.

105. Tom Friedman   Friedman is a syndicated columnist for The New York Times, multiple winner of the Pulitzer Prize and the author of best-sellers including *The Lexus and the Olive Tree* (1999), *The World Is Flat* (2005), and *Hot, Flat, and Crowded: Why We Need a Green Revolution* (2008).

105. Jennifer Aaker   Aaker is the co-author of *The Dragonfly Effect* and a professor at Stanford's School of Business where she teaches a 2-hour course. "How to Tell a Story." Check out her syllabus at http://faculty-gsb.stanford.edu/aaker/pages/documents/GSBGEN542HowtoTellaStory_Syllabus2009.pdf

106. George Orwell   Orwell published *Nineteen Eighty-Four* in 1949. (It was made into a movie with Richard Burton in—yes—1984). It and *Animal Farm* have sold more copies than any other two books by a 20th century author. Orwell was an ardent socialist.

106. Steve Jobs' 1984 video   The video that introduced the 1984 Mac was directed by Ridley Scott who also directed *Blade Runner*. Both the video and the film are considered to be ground-breaking masterpieces.

106. *The Leader's Guide to Storytelling*   Written by Stephen Denning (2005, Jossey-Bass), this book offers eight kinds of stories, each with a different purpose. The eight include stories to (1) motivate others to action, (2) build trust in you, (3) build trust in your company, (4) transmit your values, (5) get others working together, (6) share knowledge, (7) tame the grapevine, and (8) create and share your vision.

106. The springboard story   In *The Leader's Guide to Storytelling*. Denning recommends this kind of story to "ignite action and implement new ideas" (2005, Jossey-Bass, p. 18).

107. *"This question becomes important..."*   This quote is from *How to Tell a Story*, Jennifer Aaker's Stanford Graduate School of Business web page.

108. *"...if I tell the audience..."*   This quote is from *The Leader's Guide to Storytelling* by Stephen Denning (2005, Jossey-Bass, pp. 66-67).

108. Christa Ledbetter   Ledbetter is a Disability Advocate for the Center for Independent Living. This is what she did as an awareness activity to introduce a change in management.

110. *"One key area to focus on..."* This quote is from *The Leader's Guide to Storytelling* by Stephen Denning (2005, Jossey-Bass, p. 42).

Chapter 9 Change Agent Team

113. Kill the Messenger   The *Random House Dictionary of Popular Proverbs and Sayings* says, "This idea was expressed by Sophocles as far back as 442 B.C. and much later by Shakespeare in 'Henry IV, Part II' and in 'Antony and Cleopatra' (1606-07)...Originated in the United States in the Wild West, around 1860. During his 1883 tour of the United States, Oscar Wilde (1854-1900) saw this saying on a notice in a Leadville, Colorado, saloon. It is sometimes attributed to Mark Twain, but neither Wilde nor Twain has ever claimed authority.

115. Jack Welch   As CEO (1981-2001), Welch is credited with changing General Electric from a slumbering giant into a lean, competitive corporation. During his reign, GE's value went from $13 billion to several hundred bullion. He worked to eliminate bureaucracy and to reward success. His no-nonsense leadership style and his downsizing of 100,000 employees led to his getting the nickname of Neutron Jack. His personal fortune is estimated at $750,000,000.

115. "Avoid using data like a drunk..." Not sure what the original source was, but (along with a lot of other things) I learned it from Sivasailam "Thiagi" Thiagarajan, international consultant in training games. Go to thiagi.com/ for more information, as well as freebies to improve your training.

115. Sivasailam "Thiagi" Thiagarajan   An international consultant in training games. Go to thiagi.com/ for more information.

115. The Sender Matters! The Medium Matters!   These principles are derived from *Diffusion of Innovations* by Everett Rogers (2003, The Free Press).

116. *"Over the past year, the Obama campaign..."* The quote is from "The Machinery of Hope" by Tim Dickinson (*Rolling Stone*, March 20, 2008).

116. *"Everything that is done or is not done sends a message."* The quote is from "Managing Change: the Art of Balancing" by Jeanie Daniel Duck (1998, *Harvard Business Review on Change*). Another author, John Putzier, (*Get Weird*, 2001, American Management Association, pp. 68-70) cautions that, while a task force meeting that is open to all (though not necessarily as participants) can reduce resistance to change, it requires two things: "First, it requires that there be a mechanism in place that allows people to find out what meetings are scheduled and when and where they are.

Second, it implies that these meetings are open to anyone who wants to attend and can attend." This whole effort toward transparency is compatible with Ken Kovach's findings that employees value highly "being in on things" (1999, *Human Resources Development*).

117. Peter Drucker   The Ducker quote is from "The Age of Social Transformation." (*The Atlantic Monthly*, November 1994)

118. Training & Instructional design   There are many books on instructional design. One that has been lauded for being both research-based and practitioner-friendly is *Writing Training Materials that Work: How to Teach Anyone to Do Anything* by Rob Foshay, Ken Silber, and Michael Stelnicki (2003, Pfeiffer).

120. "I have often asked fishermen…"   The quote is from "Empathy, The first Key to Successful Change," a chapter in *How to Manage Change Effectively* by Donald Kirkpatrick (1985, Jossey-Bass, p. 112). He proposes three "keys to successful change"—empathy, communication, and participation—and devotes a chapter to each of them.

123. "The power one needs comes…"   The quote is from *Power and Influence: Beyond Formal Authority* by John P. Kotter (1985, The Free Press, p. 39).

124. The Wisdom of Teams   This is a well thought-of book on team-building by Jon Katzenbach and Douglas K. Smith (1993, Harvard Business School Press).

124. "A powerful guiding group…"   The quote is from *The Heart of Change* by John P. Kotter and Dan S. Cohen (2002, Harvard Business School Press, p. 43).

128. Inside-Outside Perspective   The table comparing internal and external change agents is based on descriptions in *The Change Agent's Guide to Innovation in Education* by Ronald G. Havelock (1973, Educational Technology Publications).

129. Developmental Stages of Teams   Bruce Tuckman first identified and documented the form-storm-norm-perform concept of developmental stages in 1965. Later, in *Team Players and Teamwork* (2008, Jossey-Bass), Glenn Parker applied the concept to teams, proposed four roles (contributor, collaborator, communicator, challenger) and described in detail their related concerns and actions at each of the four stages.

Chapter 10 Leadership & Participation

132. Leadership   The concept of leadership is clearly described and differentiated from management by John Kotter in *A Force for Change: How Leadership Differs From Management* (1990, The Free Press).

133. Gloria Steinem A political activist and feminist leader of the Women's Liberation Movement in the 60's and 70's. She co-founded *Ms. Magazine* and worked with Jane Fonda to co-found the Women's Media Center.

133. General George C. Patton (1885-1945) An outspoken and controversial general during WWII, he led the U.S. Third Army in France. He was made famous to later generations with George C. Scott's Academy Award winning portrayal in the 1970 film *Patton*.

133. Martin Luther King, Jr. (1929-1968) An iconic figure and charismatic speaker in the civil rights movement of the 50s and 60s, he supported the nonviolent methods of Mahatma Gandhi. In 1964, he was the youngest person to win the Nobel Peace Prize. He was assassinated on April 4, 1968.

133. Mahatma Gandhi (1869-1948) He was the political and ideological leader of India during their independence movement. His ideas of nonviolent resistance have impacted subsequent world leaders., e.g., Martin Luther King, Jr. and Nelson Mandela. He was assassinated on January 30, 1948.

133. Magic Johnson In the 80s, a much-admired basketball player for the Los Angeles Lakers, he was chosen the NBA's Most Valuable Player. He retired in 1991 after announcing that he had HIV, but returned to play and to retire twice more. He was a member of the US Dream Team that won the 1992 Olympic gold medal.

135. *"To choose a direction..."* This quote is from *Leaders: The Strategies for Taking Charge* by Warren Bennis and Burt Nanus (1985, New York: Harper and Row, p. 89).

135. Jack Welch The anecdote about doodling his vision for GE on a napkin came from *Jack Straight from the Gut* (2001, Warner Business Books, pp. 101-102).

136. *"We used to fly planes..."* The quote is by Jan Carlzon, COO of Scandinavian Airline Systems. It was cited in *A Force for Change* by John P. Kotter (1990, The Free Press).

136. Believe it—or forget it The quote is from Martin Luther King's "I have a dream" speech delivered at the Lincoln Memorial on August 28, 1963.

136. *"The first task in enlisting others..."* The quote is from *The Leadership Challenge* by James Kouzes and Barry Posner (2008, Jossey-Bass, p. 129).

137. *"We define a leader not..."* The quote is from *Reengineering the Corporation* by Michael Hammer and James Champy (2003, Harper Paperbacks, p. 109).

140. Daryl Conner The discussion of sponsors is based on two of Daryl Conner's publications—In *Managing at the Speed of Change* (1993, Villard) and *Sponsor Commitment Evaluation* (1983, OD Resources).

144. Help Your Sponsors John Kotter's eight steps for leading change provide the framework for his *Leading Change* (1996, Harvard Business School Press).

148. Power to the People The two books referenced are *The Inmates Are Running the Asylum* by Alan Cooper (2004, Sams-Pearson Education) and *User Design* by Alison Carr-Chellman (2007, Lawrence Erlbaum Associates, Inc.).

148. Example—The Usual Way The scenario described is from "Managing Change: the Art of Balancing" by Jeannie Daniel Duck in *Harvard Business Review on Change* (1998, Harvard Business School Press).

149. Example—A Better Way This is a real case with the names changed.

151. Centralized and Decentralized Approaches These concepts are described in and the quotes come from *Diffusion of Innovations* by Everett M. Rogers (2003, The Free Press, pp. 394-399).

152. Rosabeth Moss Kanter With *The Change Masters* (1985, The Free Press), Kanter was established as one of the first major theorists in the area of corporate change. The quote came from her online blog, "Seven Truths about Change to Lead By and Live By" (*Harvard Business Review*, October 11, 2010).

152. *"Pay now, or pay later."* One of the many punchy and memorable quotes from Daryl Conner. From a Conner presentation I attended in the 80s.

Chapter 11 Organization

156. How important is the organization's culture? The quotes are from Kim S. Cameron & Robert E. Quinn's *Diagnosing and Changing Organizational Culture* (2006, Jossey-Bass, p.1), Daryl Conner's *Managing at the Speed of Change* (1993, Villard), and Louis V. Gerstner's *Who Says Elephants Can't Dance?* (2003, Harper Paperbacks).

156. *"It's the way things..."* Although Terrence E. Deal & Allan A. Kennedy are usually credited with this quote, in their book, *Corporate Cultures: the Rites and Rituals of Corporate Life* (1982, Addison-Wesley. p. 4), they cite Marvin Bower, ex-managing director of McKinsey & Company as the source.

156. *"...it encompasses the taken-for-granted values..."* The quote is from *Diagnosing and Changing Organizational Culture* by Kim S. Cameron & Robert E. Quinn (2006, Jossey-Bass, p. 16).

156. *"Can you imagine..."* The quote is from *The Corporate Culture Survival Guide* by Edgar H. Schein (1999, Jossey-Bass, p. xiv).

157. *"One of the easiest ways..."* The quote is from *Images of Organization* by Gareth Morgan (2006, Sage Publications, p. 121).

157. Schein's Three Levels This section is based on *The Corporate Culture Survival Guide* by Edgar H. Schein (1999, Jossey-Bass).

158. OCAI In *Diagnosing and Changing Organizational Culture* (2006, Jossey-Bass), Kim Cameron and Robert Quinn offer the Organizational Culture Assessment Instrument (OCAI). It has been validated in more than a 1000 organizations. It is user-friendly and requires only that individuals respond to four questions regarding each of six area: dominant characteristics, organizational leadership, employee management, organization glue, strategic emphases, and success criteria. When used by a group of organizational people who share and discuss the results, it's a good team builder as well as a tool for facilitating change.

158. Multiple Cultures The White House example of multiple cultures came from a Daryl Conner presentation I attended in the 80s.

160. *"Effective managers and professionals..."* The quote is from *Images of Organization* by Gareth Morgan (2006, Sage Publications, p. 11). Morgan describes eight images briefly summarized here:

> **Machine**—Probably the oldest image and the one that was dominant in the Industrial Revolution, this image implies that organizations are "made up of interlocking parts that each play a clearly defined role in the functioning of the whole...the mechanical way of thinking is so ingrained in our everyday conceptions of organizations that it is often very difficult to organize in any other way."

> **Organism**—An image modeled after the living organism and, therefore, one that follows a relatively predictable developmental pattern over time, has needs, and interacts with its environment.

> **Brain**—An image modeled after the human brain and emerging from the computer revolution, this one sees the organization as an information processing system or hologram that has intelligence, learns and is self-organizing.

> **Culture**—An image based on the "ideas, values, norms, rituals, and beliefs that sustain organizations as socially constructed realities." (Since Morgan uses the concept of "culture" as just one of his images, he may view those who, like Schein, focus only on culture as leaving out the other images. Of course, Schein may view his concept of culture as encompassing all of Morgan's images.)

> **Political System**—An image that focuses "on the different sets of interest, conflicts, and power plays that shape organizational activity." In short, such an image implies scarce resources and, as a result, conflict.

> **Psychic Prison**—Derived from a psychoanalytical perspective, this image is based on the idea that, in an organization, "people become trapped by their own thoughts, ideas, and beliefs, or by preoccupations originating in the unconscious mind." Morgan asks, "Could it be that our favored modes of organizing

manifest an unconscious preoccupation with control? ...repressed sexuality? ...fear of death?...Could it be that our ways of organizing are designed to protect us from ourselves?"

Flux and Transformation—This image involves three different "logics of change shaping social life." One logic says "organizations are self-producing systems that create themselves in their own image. Another emphasizes how they are produced as a result of circular flows or positive and negative feedback. And a third suggests that they are the product of a dialectical logic whereby every phenomenon tends to generate its opposite."

Instrument of Domination—This image focuses on the "potentially exploitative aspects of organization" and "shows how organizations often use their employees, their host communities, and the world economy to achieve their own ends." Morgan says that this image is useful "for understanding how actions that are rational from one viewpoint can prove exploitative from another."

Some of these images (e.g., flux and transformation) are somewhat esoteric and difficult to grasp. However, if you are up to the struggle, this book is likely to change forever your understanding of organizations. In any event, the overall concept of images and metaphors is helpful in understanding the organization in which you are trying to facilitate a change project.

160. Jane V. Gallos' Classification System In *Reframing Organizations* (2003, Jossey-Bass), Lee Bolman and Terrance Deal write about frames and images and propose four categories: structural, human resource, political, and symbolic. In "Reframing Complexity," a chapter in *Organizational Development* (2006, Jossey-Bass) Jane Gallos uses their framework to describe and prescribe. The following is adapted from Gallos.

FRAME	IMAGE	DESCRIPTION	PROBLEM-SOLVING METHOD
Structural	Machine	formal roles & regulations coordination & control aligned goals, tasks, tech, environment	analyze & realign create mechanisms to integrate individual-group-unit efforts
Human Resource	Family	orgs. exist to serve people needs people & org. mutually dependent	redesign org. to meet people needs retrain people to meet org. needs
Political	Jungle	people have competing interests people compete for scarce resources	bargain, negotiate, build coalitions, manage conflict
Symbolic	Theater	meaning is more important than what happens culture holds org. together	create common vision devise rituals, symbols infuse passion, creativity, soul

161. Henry Ford (1863-1947) Founder of the Ford Motor Company, Henry Ford was responsible for the assembly line technique of mass production. While this approach contributed to industry's and the nation's economic success, the method also reduced people to functioning like parts of a machine.

161. Charlie Chaplin (1889-1977) Viewed as a genius, Chaplin's career as an actor and director began with silent films and continued for 75 years. His most famous character was the Little Tramp who was featured in, among other films, the classic *Modern Times* which pictured the struggle of an ordinary little man trying to survive in an industrial world. If you've never seen it, it's worth watching. Clips are available on YouTube.

162. Skunk works Wikipedia says, "The term 'Skunk Works' came from the Al Capp comic strip *Li'l Abner*, which was popular in the 1940s...the 'Skonk Works' was a backwoods still operated by Big Barnsmell...he made 'kickapoo joy juice' by grinding dead skunks and worn shoes into a smoldering vat." Rogers says (*Diffusion of Innovations*, 2003, p. 149) that the application of the name to R&D units came about during World War II when Lockheed's California R&D group was set up next to a plastics factory that omitted foul smells. Workers dubbed their unit a "Skunk Works" after Al Capp's still.

164. Family Image—Abraham Maslow (1908-1970) A psychologist at Brandeis University, Maslow founded humanistic psychology and, unlike many researchers, studied mentally healthy and productive people. He is best known for his Hierarchy of Needs which begins with the most basic of human needs—the physical—and continues upward through safety needs, love and belonging needs, and esteem needs and which culminates in the need for self-actualization. His theories had a significant impact on management practices.

165. Frederick the Great (1712-1786) King of Prussia, he had a turbulent upbringing. Devoted to his mother and caring about music and all things French, he was subjected by his father to a militaristic and rigid education. He once tried to escape to his mother's father, King George I of Great Britain. For this act, his father had Frederick's best friend tortured and killed. Only because of the intervention of the Kings of Sweden and Poland was young Frederick's life saved. Until his father's death, Frederick lived in isolation from the Court, but he was free to study and learn from Voltaire and others. In 1740, he became King and immediately demonstrated great military and legislative ability. After various wars, Prussia had eleven years of peace during which time Frederick improved the military, the government, and the nation as a whole. In the Seven Years War, Frederick again demonstrated his leadership, not only by winning the war, but also by doubling the size of his kingdom, filling the treasury and creating an army of 200,000.

166. *"...organization leaders must strive..."* This quote is from "Want To, Need To, Ought To" by J. T. Parish, S. Cadwallader, and P. Busch in *Journal of Organizational Change Management*. {2008, 21(1), 32-52}

Chapter 12 The Big Picture

174. Goodwin's Was 150 Years Old This is a real case with the names changed.

177. Wal-Mart From a Wal-Mart web page which has already been changed.

178. The Med-Am Case This is a real case with the names changed.

182. Sample Sociogram of a Change Project System This is based on a real case.

184. Force-Field Analysis Social psychologist Kurt Lewin(1890-1947) developed this tool to identify the forces that influence a given situation, usually a social situation. The tool emerges from Lewin's "field theory" which proposes that human behavior is a function of both the person and the environment. One online commentator, James Neill, wrote "…yoda in Star Wars brought field theory back into vogue, with his kind wish for Luke Skywalker, 'may the force [field] be with you.'"

Chapter 13 Taking Care of Yourself

188. *"Resilient people face no less…"* This quote is from *Managing at the Speed of Change* by Daryl Conner (1993, Villard, p. 65).

189. Kotter's ways of getting support from your boss These suggestions are adapted from the chapter, "Relations with Superiors: The Challenge of 'Managing' a Boss," in *Power and Influence: Beyond Formal Authority* by John P. Kotter (1985, The Free Press).

191. Take Care of Yourself These suggestions are adapted from *Transitions* by William Bridges (1980, Addison-Wesley). If you read its Amazon reviews, you will see that this book has held up for over 25 years and continues to be helpful to individuals who are facing a change—whether it be personal or work-related. A good source if you're trying to help your adopters (or yourself) get through a major change.

REFERENCES

Aaker, J., and Smith, A. *The Dragonfly Effect: Quick, Effective, and Powerful Ways to Use Social Media to Drive Social Change.* San Francisco: Jossey-Bass, 2010.

Abrahamson, E. "Change Without Pain." *Harvard Business Review,* 2005, 78(4), 75-79.

Anderson, M. B. "Interaction and Group-making in On-line Learning Communities," 1999. http://www.marshal.co.uk/telematics/articles/ws2co_op/results.htm.

Bennis, W., and Nanus, B. *Leaders.* New York: Harper Business, 1997.

Biech, E. *Thriving Through Change: A Leader's Practical Guide to Change Mastery.* Alexandria, VA: ASTD Press, 2007.

Bolman, L. G., and Deal, T. E. *Reframing Organizations: Artistry, Choice, and Leadership* (3rd ed.). San Francisco: Jossey-Bass, 2003.

Bridges, W. *Transitions: Making Sense Out of Life's Changes.* Reading, MA: Addison Wesley, 1980.

Cameron, K. S., and Quinn, R. E. *Diagnosing and Changing Organizational Culture.* San Francisco: Jossey-Bass, 2006.

Carr-Chellman, A. *User Design.* Mahwah, NJ: Lawrence Erlbaum Associates, 2007.

Chaplin, C. *Modern Times* [film], 1936.

Conner, D. R. *Managing at the Speed of Change: How Resilient Managers Succeed and Prosper Where Others Fail.* New York: Villard, 1993.

Conner, D. R. *Sponsor Commitment Evaluation.* Atlanta: OD Resources, 1983.

Cooper, A. *The Inmates Are Running the Asylum.* Indianapolis: Pearson Education, 2004.

Deal, T. E., and Kennedy, A. A. *Corporate Cultures: the Rites and Rituals of Corporate Life*. Boston: Addison-Wesley, 1982

Denning, S. *The Leader's Guide to Storytelling: Mastering the Art and Discipline of Business Narrative*. San Francisco: Jossey-Bass, 2005.

Dickinson, T. "The Machinery of Hope." *Rolling Stone*, March 20, 2008.

Drucker, P. "Managing in a Time of Great Change." *The Atlantic Monthly*, November, 1994.

Duck, J. D. "Managing Change: the Art of Balancing." *Harvard Business Review on Change*. Boston, MA: Harvard Business School Press, 1998.

Foshay, W.R., Silber, K.A., and Stelnicki, M. *Writing Training Materials That Work: How to Train Anyone to Do Anything*. San Francisco: Pfeiffer, 2003.

Friedman, T. L. *The World Is Flat*. New York: Farrar, Straus and Giroux, 2005.

Friedman, T. L. PBS *Charlie Rose Show*, August 16, 2007.

Gallos, J. V. "Reframing Complexity." In J. V. Gallos (ed.), *Organizational Development*. San Francisco: Jossey-Bass, 2006.

Gladwell, M. *The Tipping Point: How Little Things Can Make a Big Difference*. New York: Back Bay, 2000.

Gladwell, M. *Blink: The Power of Thinking Without Thinking*. New York: Back Bay, 2005.

Gladwell, M. "Small Change." *The New Yorker*, October 4, 2010.

Hall, G. E., and Hord, S. M. *Implementing Change: Patterns, Principles, and Potholes* (3rd ed.). Upper Saddle River, N. J.: Prentice Hall, 2010.

Hammer, M. and Champy, J. *Reengineering the Corporation*. New York: Harper Business, 2003.

Havelock, R. *The Change Agent's Guide*. Englewood Cliffs, N.J.: Educational Technology, 1995.

Heath, C., and Heath, D. *Switch: How to Change Things When Change Is Hard*. New York: Broadway Books, 2010.

Holmes, T., and Rahe, R. *Stress*. Blue Cross Association, 1974.

Jennings, D. "Losing a Comforting Ritual: Treatment." *New York Times*, June 30, 2009.

Johansson, H. J., McHugh, P., Pendlebury, A. J., and Wheeler, W. A. III. *Business Process Reengineering*. Hoboken, NJ: John Willey, 1994.

Kanter, B., and Fine, A.H. *The Networked Nonprofit: Connecting with Social Media to Drive Change*. San Francisco: Jossey-Bass, 2010.

Kanter, R. M. *The Change Masters*. New York: The Free Press, 1985.

Kanter, R. M. Seven Truths about Change to Lead By and Live By. *Harvard Business Review*, October 11, 2010. ttp://blogs.hbr.org/kanter/2010/08/seven-truths-about-change-to-l.html

Katzenbach, J. R., and Smith, D. K. *The Wisdom of Teams*. Boston: Harvard Business School Press, 1993.

Kirkpatrick. D. L. *How to Manage Change Effectively*. San Francisco: Jossey-Bass, 1985.

Kotler. P. *Principles of Marketing*. Upper Saddle River, N.J.: Prentice Hall, 2009.

Kotter, J. P. *Power and Influence: Beyond Formal Authority*. New York: The Free Press, 1985.

Kotter, J. P. *A Force for Change: How Leadership Differs from Management*. New York: The Free Press, 1990.

Kotter. J. P. *Leading Change*. Boston: Harvard Business School Press, 1996.

Kotter, J. P., and Cohen, D. S. *The Heart of Change: Real-life Stories of How People Change Their Organizations.* Boston: Harvard Business School Press, 2002.

Kouzes, J. M., and Posner, B. Z. *The Leadership Challenge.* San Francisco: Jossey-Bass, 1990.

Kovach, K. Employee motivation: Addressing a crucial factor in your organization's performance. *Human Resource Development.* http://edis.ifas.ufl.edu/HR017, 1999.

Kubler-Ross, E. *On Death and Dying.* New York: Macmillan, 1969.

Lewin, K. *Field Theory in Social Science; Selected Theoretical Papers.* D. Cartwright (ed.). New York: Harper & Row, 1951.

Mager, R. F. and Pipe. P. *Analyzing Performance Problems: Or You Really Oughta Wanna—How to Figure Out Why People Aren't Doing What They Should Be, and what to Do About It.* Atlanta: Center for Effective Performance, 1997.

Maurer, R. *Beyond the Wall of Resistance.* Austin: Bard Press, 1996.

McKee, R. *Story: Substance, Structure Style, and the Principles of Screenwriting.* New York: Regan Books, 1997.

Miller, R. B., Heiman, S. E. and Tuleja, T. *The New Strategic Selling.* New York: Warner Business Books, 2005.

Moore, G. A. *Crossing the Chasm: Marketing and Selling Disruptive Products to Mainstream Customers.* New York: Collins Business Essentials, 2002.

Morgan, G. *Images of Organization.* San Francisco: Berrett-Koehler, 1998.

Nadler, D.A., Gerstein, M.S., Shaw, R. B., and Associates. *Discontinuous Change: Leading Organizational Transformation.* San Francisco: Jossey-Bass, 1995.

Nelson, B. *1001 Ways to Reward Employees*. New York: Workman, 2005.

Orwell, G. *Nineteen Eighty-Four*. New York: Plume, 1949, 2003.

Parish, J. T., Cadwallader, S., and Busch, P. "Want To, Need To, Ought To: Employee Commitment to Organizational Change." *Journal of Organizational Change Management*, 2008, 21(1), 32-52.

Parker, G. M. *Team Players and Teamwork*. San Francisco: Jossey-Bass, 2008.

Rogers, E. M. *Diffusion of Innovations* (5th ed.). New York: Free Press, 2003.

Schein, E. H. *The Corporate Culture Survival Guide*. San Francisco: Jossey-Bass, 1999.

Schein, E. H. 'Kurt Lewin's Change Theory in the Field and in the Classroom: Notes Toward a Model of Managed Learning." *Systems Practice, 1995*.

Silverman, L. *Wake Me Up When the Data Is Over*. San Francisco: Jossey-Bass, 2006.

Walsh, B. "Eating Bugs." *Time Magazine*, May 29, 2008

Welch, J. *Jack Straight from the Gut*. New York: Warner, 2001.

Zaltman, G. and Duncan, R. *Strategies for Planned Change*. New York: John Wiley, 1977.

Zandt, D. *Share This! How You Will Change the World with Social Networking*. San Francisco: Berrett-Koehler, 2010.

INDEX

About the Illustrator—Joe Lee

Joe Lee received a degree in medieval history from Indiana University,. After that, he did a year of graduate work at the Ringling Brothers, Barnum and Bailey Clown College, worked for the King-Brothers-Cole Circus and the Hoxie Brothers, and did spot dates with the Big Apple Circus as a fire eater. Then he moved to New York City where, in front of the Metropolitan Museum, he sold postcards of his ink drawings. One day a young woman on roller skates stopped to admire his work and suggested he learn to etch. She took him to the Art Student's League, where he became a student and stayed to become an assistant instructor. Eventually, he returned to Bloomington, Indiana, where he now lives with his wife Bess and his son Brandon. He has illustrated books about Jung, Postmodernism, Shakespeare, and Eastern Philosophy, as well as *Dante for Beginners*, which he also wrote.

Website: joeleeillustrator.com/

About the Graphics Designer—Carol Rhodes

Carol Rhodes is a graphic design instructor/developer for IT Training at Indiana University and a member of the National Association of Photoshop Professionals. For 15 years, she has taught graduate, undergraduate, and non-credit graphic and design courses for IU and the community. Her professional efforts focus on the Adobe Creative Suite. She is also an active watercolor artist, a freelance page and web designer, and an active member on the board of Pets Alive, Inc., a regional nonprofit spay/neuter clinic. Beyond this, she confers her care and attention on her family (including a dog and too many cats), her home, and a bevy of wild birds. She tries hard to stay on top of happenings in this changing world. She cherishes many talented friends and believes each one probably experiences her in a different way.

Website: carolrhodes.net/
See her technical posts on ittrainingtips.iu.edu/

About the Author—Diane Dormant

For three decades, Diane directed Dormant & Associates, Inc. which specialized in instructional and communications projects—all of which were influenced by a change management perspective. In addition to corporate project work, she and her colleagues presented change workshops for Eli Lilly Pharmaceuticals, Toyota, Delphi-Delco, Country Insurance, US Army TRADOC, Canadian Forces TDOs as well as for various healthcare, educational and not-for-profit organizations.

Since 1984, she has taught graduate courses at Indiana University, Boise State University, and Ithaca College. Topics include change management, organizational consulting, organizational culture, and group training techniques.

She is a Past President of the International Society for Performance Improvement. She has a Ph.D. in Instructional Systems Technology from Indiana University and an M.A. in Psychology and a B.A. in English from the University of Houston.

Diane lives in Bloomington, Indiana. She teaches online and does an occasional *Chocolate Model Workshop*. She has two sons, Charlie and Julian Henry, and two grandsons, Chama and Zachariah Henry.

She can be reached at dormant@chocochange.com

Photograph by Juliet Frey

Made in the USA
Coppell, TX
15 January 2020